READING
Triumphs

D0838244

Macmillan McGraw-Hill

RFB&D
learning through listening

Students with print disabilities may be eligible to obtain an accessible, audio version of the pupil edition of this textbook. Please call Recording for the Blind & Dyslexic at 1-800-221-4792 for complete information.

A

The McGraw·Hill Companies

Mc Graw Hill **Macmillan McGraw-Hill**

Published by Macmillan/McGraw-Hill, of McGraw-Hill Education, a division of
The McGraw-Hill Companies, Inc., Two Penn Plaza, New York, New York 10121.

Printed in the United States of America

ISBN 0-02-192021-4
1 2 3 4 5 6 7 8 9 071 09 08 07 06 05

CONTENTS

Unit 1

Short vowels /a/a, /e/e, /i/i, /o/o, /u/u; Character and Plot 6
~ Fred Jumps! 7

Dan Can Rap! 8

Long vowels /ā/a_e, /ē/e_e, /ī/i_e, /ō/o_e, /ū/u_e; Plot and Setting 18
~ A Home for Nat 19

Jane Wins a Job 20

Digraphs /th/th, /sh/sh, /hw/wh, /f/ph; Compare and Contrast 30
~ Reptiles! 31

Do They Make You Shudder and Shake? 32

Long /ē/e, ee, ea; Summarize 42
~ Living On Mars 43

Seeing Mars 44

Long /ā/a, ai, ay; Cause and Effect 54
~ Lain in Pain 55

Ray and Blaine Save the Day 56

Unit 2

Long /ī/i, y, igh; Make Inferences 66
~ High on a Perch 67

The Problem With Sy 68

Soft consonants /s/c, /j/g; Main Idea and Details 78
~ Saving Trees 79

Large Trees With Large Jobs 80

Digraphs /ch/ch, tch; Main Idea and Details 90
~ Fighting for Kids 91

Which Way to Freedom? 92

Long /ō/o, oa; Problem and Solution 102
~ Finding Tony's Nose 103

Joan's First Parade 104

Diphthong /ou/ow, ou; Make Inferences 114
~ Doc Holliday 115

A Cowboy's Life 116

Unit 3

Variant vowel /ü/oo; Draw Conclusions 126
  ~ Patriot of the Sea 127
A Ride in the Moonlight 128

r-Controlled vowels /är/ar; Fact and Opinion 138
  ~ Standing Up for Their Rights 139
Susan B. Anthony: Making Her Mark on the Women's Rights Movement 140

r-Controlled vowels /ôr/or, ore; Fact and Opinion 150
  ~ Camping at Yellowstone 151
A Place for Us to Breathe 152

r-Controlled vowels /ûr/er, ir, ur; Compare and Contrast 162
  ~ What Will Turn Up? 163
A Desert Vacation 164

Silent consonants /n/kn, /r/wr, /m/mb; Draw Conclusions 174
  ~ Tony the Pilot 175
Hope's Trip to Planet Wren 176

Unit 4

Diphthong /oi/oi, oy; Character and Setting 186
  ~ My Brave Uncle 187
Grandpop's Brave Choice 188

Schwa /əl/el, le; Author's Purpose 198
  ~ Watch Out for Little Animals 199
Big Ideas for Little Animals 200

Variant vowels /ô/au, aw, /ôl/al; Make Generalizations 210
  ~ What is Democracy? 211
A New Government 212

Long /ō/o, oa, ow; Description 222
  ~ Stuck in the Snow 223
Follow the Weather 224

Variant vowels /ủ/oo; Author's Purpose 234
  ~ I'm the Best! 235
Brook's Vase of Good Thoughts 236

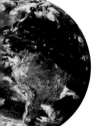

Unit 5

Review long /ā/, short /a/; Problem and Solution 246
~ A Rescue in Antarctica 247
The Loneliest Place on Earth 248

Review long /ī/, short /i/; Theme 258
~ Miserable Mike 259
The Perfect Ingredient 260

Review long /ē/, short /e/; Cause and Effect 270
~ Funny Ways to Feel Better 271
Plants That Can Heal 272

Review long /ō/, short /o/; Evaluate Author's Perspective 282
~ Pirate Molly Does a Good Job 283
Joe and Nicole Crack the Code 284

Review variant vowels /ů/oo, /ü/oo; Summarize 294
~ The Lesson 295
Proof of Goodness 296

Unit 6

r-Controlled vowels; Identify Sequence of Events 306
~ Caught In the Act 307
The Girl Who Talked to Animals 308

Review diphthongs /ou/ow, ou; Make Judgments 318
~ A Lot to Learn 319
An Outdoor Adventure 320

Review digraphs; Identify Techniques of Persuasion 330
~ Stopping a Bully 331
The Truth About Bullies 332

Review long and short vowels; Make Generalizations 342
~ Fly Far, Fly Safely 343
Up, Up, and Away!!! 344

Review long and short vowels; Identify Sequence of Events 354
~ The Sinking of the Titanic 355
Alvin: Underwater Exploration 356

Skills and Strategies

Decoding

Decode these words. What do you notice about the spellings?

clap	spot	tin	desk
miss	slap	pals	next
luck	trust	grand	contest

Vocabulary

gasps	on edge	worried
slips	hand	nervous

Comprehension

CHARACTER AND PLOT

A character is a person or animal in the story.

Character	Plot

The plot is made up of the events that happen in the story. The plot includes a problem, a way to solve the problem, and the solution.

A Character and Plot Chart helps you figure out a character's personality and the events of the plot.

Identify the characters and plot in the passage.

Fred Jumps!

Fred can jump fast. His mom and dad see him jump, and they gasp. "You can jump so fast!" they tell him.

Miss Tab tells Fred's class that she will test how fast they can jump. Fred is on edge. He has never jumped with so many pals. He is worried he will trip. He wants to slip away.

He gets set to run and jump fast. Miss Tab yells, "Jump!" Fred jumps as fast as he can. He wins! His class gives him a hand. Now when Fred jumps, he will not get nervous. He will jump the best that he can!

Make a **Character and Plot Chart** for "Fred Jumps!". Use it to help you summarize the story.

Dan Can Rap!

by Alexi Brown

illustrated by
Tomoko Watanabe

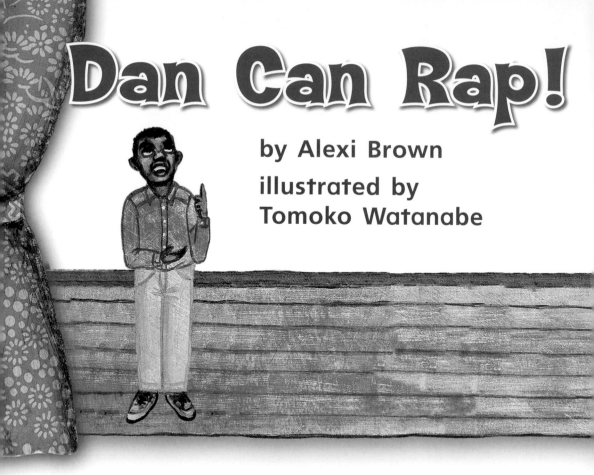

A Big Win!

Dan's class can tell he is in the hall before they see him. He raps as he passes in the hall. Dan raps as he slips into class. And Dan raps as he sits at his desk.

Dan is in a rap contest at school. When Dan raps, his pals will clap. The kids think his rapping is grand. But can Dan win?

Dan did win! He got the top spot!

Back in class, Dan's pals give him a big hand. "Dan is a star in our class!" Mal says.

Ben stands up and slaps Dan's hand. "That was grand, Dan. You are a champ!"

Miss Mills says, "Dan did win! His next step is to rap on *American Rap Star* on TV. We can all give Dan a big hand."

Miss Mills grins. The class claps and yells for Dan.

Miss Mills and his class are thrilled, but Dan sinks in his desk. Dan cannot rap on TV. Dan is afraid to rap in a big place.

In class, Dan cannot do his math. Dan cannot think. Dan is not a kid who gets nervous a lot, but he does not wish to sing on TV.

He's Our Champ!

The sign reads: "Dan, Good Luck on *American Rap Star!*"

When Dan gets to class the next day, he sees a sign on a wall. It says, "Dan, Good Luck on *American Rap Star!*" Dan thinks he will quit. Then he will not have to rap on TV.

Dan's Pals Have a Plan

Dan's pals can tell he is on edge.

At the end of the day, Mal calls up Nick. Mal says, "I think Dan will quit the rap contest."

Nick thinks Mal is right. Nick and Mal will make a plan to help Dan.

Nick says, "In class, we will ask the rest of Dan's pals to help us, too."

Dan's pals plan to give him a tip. The kids will give Dan a picture of his class. They will tell him to set it on a stand. When Dan raps on TV he can look at the picture. Then he can think that he is just rapping for them.

The contest is the next day. Dan is set to go. Dan is not worried any more. Nick grabs him in the hall to wish him good luck. Nick says, "I wish I could rap like you, Dan! You are the best rapper! Can you help me rap some day?"

"That's a grand plan!" gasps Dan.

At the contest, the man calls Dan's name, and Dan runs on stage. The crowd is big! Dan gets nervous. He thinks he cannot rap in front of such a big crowd.

Then Dan thinks of his class. He will think of singing just for them. Dan sets the picture on the stand.

The picture does the trick! Dan sings his rap. Dan sings well. The crowd claps and yells. Dan did it!

Comprehension Check

Summarize

Read "Dan Can Rap!" again.
Fill in the Character and Plot
Chart, and then use it to
summarize the story.

Character	Plot

Think About It

1. How did Dan feel about singing on TV?
   How do you know?
2. How did Mal and Nick know that Dan was
   not happy?
3. What might be some other ways you would
   have helped Dan if he were your pal?
4. What can we tell about Dan's pals? What
   kind of people are they?

Write About It

What makes people want to quit? What are
some reasons that people do not quit even
when they want to? Explain a time when you
wanted to quit.

Skills and Strategies

Decoding

Decode these words. What do you notice about the spellings?

sled	bone	tale	mile
smoke	pink	save	pride
name	stuck	plant	sunset

Vocabulary

awoke	create	logging
enormous	smokestack	

Comprehension

PLOT AND SETTING The plot is a series of events that happen in a story. The setting of a story is when and where the events take place.

Plot	Setting

A Plot and Setting Chart helps you identify why the setting is important to the plot of the story.

Identify the plot and setting.

A Home for Nat

Sleeping in the woods far from his home, Nat got cold. He awoke and rubbed his hands together. "I will create a home here so I will not be cold," said Nat.

Nat's pal, Tim, planned to help with the logging. So Nat and Tim made Nat an enormous home. Tim cut up trees and Nat stuck logs together.

"I want a smokestack on my home," said Nat. So Nat and Tim made a smokestack. They went into the home. It was just how Nat liked it, hot. Nat was happy with his home in the woods.

Make a **Plot and Setting Chart** for "A Home for Nat." Find out how the setting effects the plot.

Jane Wins a Job

by Jennifer Notarangelo
illustrated by
Dana Trattner

Paul Bunyan is the king of lumberjacks. His job is to cut tall trees. It is the best job for him because he is a mile long! Paul can create a log cabin in a snap.

But did you know that Paul is a dad? He has a kid named Jane. She is big, just like her dad.

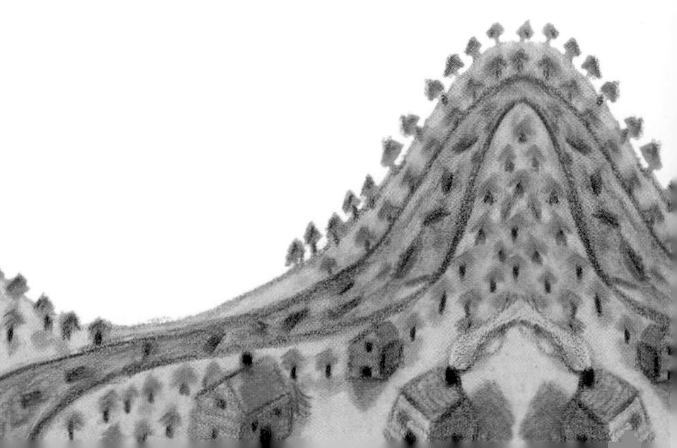

When Jane was a tot, she was a lot bigger than her pals. Jane was so huge that she played in three states at the same time.

As Jane got bigger, she chose to work with her dad. She liked to plant and dig with him and his men. This tale tells how Jane saved the day for them.

Jane Spots a Problem

At the end of a long day of cutting and logging, Paul and his men got tired. The sun was setting and his men had to rest. But there was no log cabin that could fit so many of them.

Jane had a plan to help. "Dad, you are a lumberjack. You can chop trees to make a log cabin for your men. Then you can make sure the log cabin will be big. It has to fit all of the men."

"That is a grand plan!" Paul said.

Paul and his men cut trees for the enormous log cabin. It was finished by sunset. The men were glad to get in bed. They fell fast asleep in the bunk beds.

The next day, the men awoke and became nervous. The sun did not look right. Was it stuck?

Jane Lends a Hand

Most of the men went to work cutting and planting. Some stayed to see if there was a problem.

There was a problem. The sun was stuck! It could not pass over the big log cabin. The men got more and more nervous.

"Let's talk to Jane. She helped us before. I bet she can fix this."

The other men thought so, too. They stopped work and went to ask Jane.

"Can you help us, Jane? The sun is stuck. It is in front of the smokestack on top of our log cabin. Can you fix the problem?"

Jane did a lot of thinking. She came up with a plan. If she held the smokestack down, the sun could pass over it. Then the log cabin would be safe.

Jane put her hair up and got a workshirt to wear. She tugged at the smokestack with all her might. It bent over and rested on top of the roof.

The sun rose over the log cabin and went across the sky. Jane's big plan had worked. The men gasped. They were glad the log cabin was safe. Jane had saved the day.

It made Paul smile. He had a lot of pride in Jane. He made Jane his top helper.

Comprehension Check

Summarize

Read "Jane Wins a Job" again. Fill in your Plot and Setting Chart as you read, and then use it to summarize the story.

Plot	Setting

Think About It

1. What was the first problem Jane solved? How was the problem related to the story's setting?
2. Why did the men need a new cabin?
3. Would you like to know someone like Jane? Explain your answer.
4. What are some other ways that Jane and the men could have solved the problem?

Write About It

Think about a problem that was solved in school. How was it solved? What happened as a result?

Skills and Strategies

Decoding

Decode these words. What do you notice about the spellings?

phone	fish	shade	think
while	phase	whale	whisker
path	crush	graph	whimper

Vocabulary

| reptile | prey | victim |
| venom | stun | |

Comprehension

COMPARE AND CONTRAST To compare two things, we think about how they are alike. To contrast them, we think about how they are different.

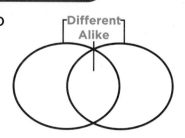

A Venn Diagram shows what is alike and what is different. Use your Venn Diagram to compare and contrast things in the story.

Compare and contrast alligators and snakes.

Reptiles!

Alligators are neat reptiles. They use camouflage to hide, just like snakes! Resting in the water, an alligator seems to be a log!

Alligators are cold-blooded, just like snakes. When the sun sets, they wake up and wait for prey. While snakes kill with venom, an alligator does not. It does not stun its prey before it eats it. It just uses its teeth to eat its victims whole!

It is a great triumph to catch a big alligator. People stuff them as trophies to show they are brave.

Make a **Venn Diagram** for "Reptiles!" Use it to explain how snakes and alligators are alike and how they are different.

Do They Make You Shudder and Shake?

by Kate Lindsey

Scales and Fangs

It can slide on flat land, slip in grass, and swim in a lake. It makes a home in hot spots and slithers away if you get too close. What is it? It is a snake. But do not shudder! Do not shake! Get more facts on this reptile.

This may look like a worm, but it's really a tiny snake.

A snake is long and thin and has no legs. Snakes can be enormous. They can grow more than thirty feet long. That is longer than a big bus! Snakes can also be small and fit in a kid's hand.

Big snakes can weigh as much as a small horse!

A snake is a reptile, and reptiles are cold-blooded. A snake is as cold or hot as the air around it. Cold days make snakes move slowly. Snakes warm up by resting in sunshine.

Snakes stay warm by taking rests on rocks in the sun.

This snake is hiding. If it blends in well, both enemies and victims will not know it's there.

Snakes do not have flesh like us. Snake skin shines and seems wet, but it is made up of dry scales. Snake scales can be different colors.

A lot of snakes are the same colors as the land around them. They are camouflaged. This helps snakes hide from things that can eat them. Snakes with poison have blazing colors. This is a danger signal. It tells animals to get away or risk a bite.

A snake is always growing, but its skin is not. One phase of growth is when the snake creates a new skin and sheds its old skin. It can shed up to 18 times in a year! To shed its old skin a snake rubs on a rough rock or a twig. Then it slides out, and the skin it sheds is left inside out.

This snake is shedding its skin. It rubs itself on rocks and sticks to make its skin slip off.

A snake finds food by flicking its tongue to taste dust in the air.

Snake Bite!

Snakes can not hear or see well. A snake sticks out its tongue so it can taste and smell the dust in the air. Dust tells a snake if it is close to its prey.

Snakes can strike in a flash and eat their prey whole. They like to eat small animals, like rats. A snake can wait for a rat to pass it. A snake can also slink up behind its victim and bite it!

Look! A snake just ate an egg.

Inside the snake, the egg will get pressed until it cracks. The snake will eat the inside of the egg. Then the snake will crush the egg shell. It will spit up the shell. The shell will be flat and thin when the snake spits it up.

If a snake is very big, it can eat a whole deer in one sitting.

A snake's fangs are tucked up inside its mouth. When it prepares to strike, it bares its fangs.

A snake has teeth and will bite if it is scared. A snake opens its mouth to bite and stun its enemy.

Snakes with poison have fangs. Fangs will prick the skin like needles. Then the fangs pass venom into the snake's prey. Venom is like poison and can make the prey ill or kill it.

Sea snakes have a flat tail that helps them swim fast. They can hold their breath for a long time while swimming under water.

Many people do not like snakes. They think that all snakes will hurt them. But snakes are scared of people. If you get close, snakes will usually slip quickly to a safe spot.

Snakes have a special place in nature. They help keep animal pests, like rats, away. So we do not have to shudder and shake every time we see a snake!

Comprehension Check

Summarize

Read "Do They Make You Shudder and Shake?" again. Then summarize the story.

Think About It

1. Tell how poisonous snakes compare to non-poisonous snakes. Use details from the story.

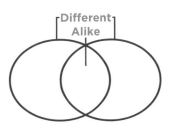

2. Why are so many people afraid of snakes?

3. What new fact did you learn about snakes?

4. Reread "Dan Can Rap!" How is Dan's fear similar to a fear of snakes? How is it different?

Write About It

Write to explain why people should not fear snakes.

Skills and Strategies

Decoding

Decode these words. What do you notice about the spellings?

seek	feet	peak	thank
gleam	whine	neat	seem
shade	below	beneath	easy

Vocabulary

orbits   gravity   volcano
object

Comprehension

SUMMARIZE A summary is a short statement that tells the most important ideas in a selection.

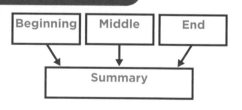

To help you write a summary for a selection, make a Summary Chart.

Summarize the passage.

Living on Mars

Living on Mars would not be easy. Earth and Mars orbit the same sun. But Mars takes longer to spin on its axis than Earth. That means days are longer on Mars.

Making a home on Mars seems tricky. Mars has less gravity so light objects might float away! We might feel very cold if we lived there. And big volcanoes can explode at any time!

Living on Mars is not yet safe. One day, we hope that we will be able to make homes on Mars.

Make a **Summary Chart** for "Living on Mars." Fill in each part as you read. Then use the chart to write a short summary of the selection in your own words.

Seeing Mars

by Amy Sweeten

What is in that wide space in the sky? At night, you can see stars shine. With luck, you can see planets.

A planet that can be seen with the naked eye is Mars. Mars **orbits** the sun in a path near Earth. We can take a peek at Mars to try to unlock its secrets!

Mars is half as big as Earth and very far away, but it can be seen on a clear night.

A Peek at Mars...

There are nine planets. Earth is the third planet from the sun. It is 93 million miles away. Mars is the fourth planet from the sun and 142 million miles away.

A day on Mars seems the same as on Earth. Mars takes just 37 minutes longer to spin on its axis than Earth does. But it takes Mars twice as long to orbit the sun as it takes Earth. That's why a year on Mars is about twice as long as a year on Earth.

Moons with Greek Names

Mars has two moons Phobos (FO•bos) and Deimos (DEE•mos). The Greek names mean "fear" and "panic." Each moon is small in size and has an odd shape.

The Red Planet

Mars is half the size of Earth. To us, it seems like a red dot in the sky. Mars gets called the Red Planet.

Is it in flames? Is it a red hot place? No, Mars appears red because it is covered in iron oxide dust. During a dust storm, "rust dust" is whipped up and Mars seems to gleam red.

The land on Mars seems red and hot. Mars is not hot at all!

It is not a hot blaze that makes Mars seem red. In fact, it can be quite cold. In some places it can be less than -200°F. Mars has frozen icecaps at the north and south poles, just like Earth does.

Mars has an enormous volcano, just like those on Earth. Its peak is a stunning 13.6 miles high. The tallest volcano peak on Earth is 2.6 miles!

The volcano, Olympus Mons, is three times as big as the biggest mountain on Earth.

This is not a gleaming star. It is Mars!

Can We Breathe on Mars?

Could we spend a lot of time on Mars? Mars is full of red rocks and dust. It has icecaps and tall peaks. Earth has them too. But Mars is quite unlike Earth.

There is no water on Mars that can be seen. It has no lakes, streams, or seas. The air on Mars is too thin to breathe.

Mars has less gravity than Earth does. The men in this spaceship have no gravity to hold them down.

Another problem with life on Mars is gravity. That is what keeps an object on land. Mars does not have much of it. While on Mars, you would weigh less than half of what you weigh on Earth. A lack of gravity will make you sick.

Fleets of Spaceships and Robots

Mars may not seem to invite us. But it has one thing that can make us smile. Mars has a face that keeps smiling back at us!

Do you see what I see? Rocks on Mars seem just like a face.

If we keep reading about Mars we will know more. Maybe at a future date, it will be safe for us to go there. Until then, spaceships and robots will be created and sent to Mars. They can report back with data and pictures. They can help reveal Mars' secrets!

Only half of the empty spaceships and robots sent to Mars have landed safely. One day, if it is safe, we may send people as well.

Comprehension Check

Summarize

Read "Seeing Mars" again. Fill in your chart, and use it to summarize the story.

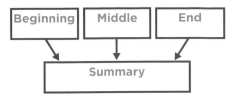

Think About It

1. Why is Mars called the Red Planet?
2 Why might the dust on Mars be called *rust dust?*
3. What is one thing you learned about Mars that surprised you? Explain your answer.
4. Do you think it's a good idea to send robots to Mars right now instead of people? Why or why not?

Write About It

Think about what it would be like to travel to Mars. Write a short story about being the first person to visit Mars. Include details from the selection about the planet.

Skills and Strategies

Decoding

Decode these words. What do you notice about the spellings?

pain	gray	feet	fail
stay	claim	trail	day
teeth	tray	chain	year

Vocabulary

supplies	beam	recover
plea	cure	dismay

Comprehension

CAUSE AND EFFECT A cause is something that makes an action happen. The action that happens as a result of the cause is the effect.

Cause ➜ Effect
➜
➜
➜
➜

A Cause and Effect Chart helps you ask questions to figure out what happens in a story (an effect) and why it happens (a cause).

Identify the causes and effects.

Lain in Pain

One day, Lain was on his way to get supplies from a shop. Lain's face beamed as he rode down a big hill. But, then he fell off of his bike. He sprained his foot and hurt his leg. His dad took him home to recover.

Lain's leg hurt a lot. He made a plea to get the pain to stop. His dad went to a store to find a cure for the pain. The store did not have it. Then Lain's mom came home with the cure she got at the hospital. It helped, but to Lain's dismay, he still had to stay in bed for a week!

Make a **Cause and Effect Chart**. Use it to help you find the causes and effects in "Lain in Pain."

Ray and Blaine Save the Day

by Julia McDonald
illustrated by Maureen Zimdars

A Plea for Help

Dean and Heath awoke when Dr. Aiken poked his head in. He made a funny joke as he checked in on the kids, but it did not cheer them up at all.

"Each bone in my body is in pain," whined Heath. Dean nodded. He felt the same way.

Dr. Aiken rushed to the phone and called the drug store. The man at the drug store was unable to help.

"If I had the pills, I would help," he said. "There was a mistake. Supplies failed to come this week. And with a big storm on the way, I do not think any more will be in soon."

Dr. Aiken hung up in dismay. He needed a new plan.

Dr. Aiken picked up the phone again. He waited as it rang. Then he began to beam. He heard Ray pick up on the other end.

"Hi, Ray. This is Dr. Aiken. I am calling with a plea for help."

Ray made his home in a big city, miles away. That city had a big hospital. Dr. Aiken knew the hospital would have the pills Dean and Heath needed. He told Ray about his problem.

"We can help! A few flakes cannot stop my dogs," Ray stated with pride. "We will bring what you need."

Ray raced sled dogs. Ray and his dogs had been on trails in a lot of bad storms. Ray rode while the dogs dragged the sled.

Ray planned for the trip. He went to the hospital and got the medicine. The storm was big, but Ray was not worried. He knew his dogs could make it.

Blaine Leads the Way

The sky was still gray and dim the next day as Ray and his dogs got set to go. Ray slipped the cure into his sack.

Three feet of new white snow were on the land. Spots of ice made the trip slippery, and it was very cold. But the dogs' thick fur kept them warm.

With Blaine leading the way, the dog team was fast. They kept the same pace and ran together. They had a quick rest late in the day and then kept running. They aimed to get the cure into Dr. Aiken's hands that same day.

Dr. Aiken went inside just as Dad was making a snack for the kids.

"Are the kids feeling better?" asked Dr. Aiken.

Dad did not have time to say anything. Dad and Dr. Aiken could hear dogs yapping outside. It was a hint that Ray had made it. Dr. Aiken ran to meet him.

Ray gave the pills to Dr. Aiken. Dr. Aiken ran inside and gave them to the kids.

"The kids will recover fast," Dr. Aiken told Mom and Dad. "But they need to stay in bed for at least a week. Then they will be fine."

"We must thank Ray and his dogs. They saved Dean and Heath!" said Dad.

Comprehension Check

Summarize

Read "Ray and Blaine Save the Day" again.
Then summarize the story.

Think About It

1. Why did Dr. Aiken need Ray's
   help? Fill in your Cause and
   Effect Chart to help you.
2. What did Dr. Aiken think would
   happen if the boys didn't get
   medicine?

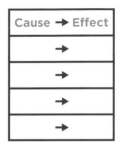

3. How have you helped someone when they
   needed help? Tell what you did.
4. Explain how Ray and the dogs were important
   to the story.

Write About It

Imagine that you are a sled dog racer, just like
Ray. What would you have done in a similar
situation? Explain your decision.

Skills and Strategies

Decoding

Decode these words. What do you notice about the spellings?

rain	high	wait	sly
sight	type	night	mind
might	shy	nearby	delight

Vocabulary

perch	fright	fierce
escapes	trembling	

Comprehension

MAKE INFERENCES

To make an inference you take clues from the story and combine them with information

Text Clues	What You Know	Inferences

you already know. This helps you monitor your understanding.

To help you make inferences, use an Inferences Chart.

Make inferences about the way birds and cats act.

High on a Perch

Animals such as birds and cats like to go up in trees. Birds make nests high on branches. A bird can sing on a perch and take care of their eggs. When a cat is nearby, birds fly away in fright!

Cats might seem fierce and sly when chasing birds. But if a cat catches sight of a dog, the cat quickly escapes to a tree. A cat can wait all night trembling on a perch until it is safe to get down. That is why it is wise to keep a cat inside.

Make an **Inferences Chart** for "High on a Perch." Use it to help you make inferences about birds and cats.

The Problem With Sy

by Marge Hoff

illustrated by Shelly Shinjo

Way Up High

Twyla slid the glass door open and peeked up at the gray sky. She sighed. It looked like it might rain.

As Twyla came back inside, a tan cat leaped up on a seat.

"Hi, Sy!" Twyla called. She picked up the cat and set him back on the floor. Twyla smiled as her pet jumped and ran behind a plant. When Twyla sat down to eat, she did not see Sy run for the sliding door.

Just as Twyla finished her meal, she heard a fierce barking and then a shrill hiss. Twyla jumped up and saw that she had not closed the door.

A shocking sight greeted Twyla. A big dog with big teeth stood on its back legs. Twyla's mind raced as she saw her cat dash to safety high in a treetop.

"Sy!" Twyla cried and ran with fright.

"I am sorry my dog gave your cat a fright!" a man yelled. He tugged on the dog's leash and dragged him back.

Twyla spoke to the shaking cat, hoping to get him to jump back down. It did not work. Sy would not leave the branch he was sitting on. Twyla ran to get a ladder. Twyla's mom came to help. They lifted the ladder up and leaned it on the tree.

Mrs. Bind stepped up the ladder. Then she held out her hands to the trembling cat.

"Come here, Sy!" she pleaded. Sy stayed on his perch.

Twyla's face fell in dismay. Mrs. Bind climbed back down and hugged Twyla. "Sy will come down when he is hungry. We will just have to wait."

Twyla spent the morning watching her cat. Then, she called her pal Brian on the phone. "Sy is up in a tree, and he will not get down. I don't know what to do," she said.

"When my cat escapes, I set a treat on the back steps," said Brian. "I will come over and help."

A Plea for Help

Twyla and Brian put out fish and waited. But Sy stayed up in the tree. Not even the hawk right by the tree could make Sy move.

The day dragged by. But as long as there was daylight, Twyla felt some hope.

As night got closer, Twyla had to go home. She was full of fright for Sy. He must be cold. Also, he had not had a bite to eat that whole day.

"Sy will be fine," Mrs. Bind said. "He has thick fur to keep him warm at night."

When Twyla climbed into bed, she knew it would be difficult to sleep. She liked Sy sleeping at the end of her bed each night.

The next day, Sy was still in the tree. Twyla heard his cries. She saw the gray sky. It would rain soon.

Twyla saw a man get out of a big truck and begin to fix a phone line. He got into a tub that lifted him up high.

Twyla made a plan. She raced outside and waved to the man in the tub. Twyla told him about Sy. The man gave her a bright smile. He lifted the tub to the cat. Sy leaped into his arms!

The man came down and handed the cat to Twyla.

"Sy, you are safe!" Twyla yelled.

Twyla beamed at the man. "Thank you, sir, for saving my cat!" she said.

"You're welcome. I am glad he is unhurt!" said the man. He waved and went back to work.

Twyla ran into the house just as it began to rain. She smiled, happy to have Sy home at last.

Comprehension Check

Summarize

Read "The Problem with Sy" again. Then summarize the story.

Think About It

1. How does Twyla feel about Sy? How do you know? Fill in the Inferences Chart to help you find inferences.

Text Clues	What You Know	Inferences

2. Why do you think Sy would not climb down the tree?
3. Would you have been worried if your pet was stuck in a tree? Why or why not?
4. How do you think the story would have been different if Sy had been a dog?

Write About It

What are some ways to keep a pet safe? Why is this important?

Skills and Strategies

Decoding

Decode these words. What do you notice about the spellings?

place	page	mile	cage
wild	large	cent	germ
space	tight	face	huge

Vocabulary

concerned	disputes	protect
gems	ripen	

Comprehension

MAIN IDEA AND DETAILS The main idea is the most important point an author makes about a topic. The details help to explain and support the main idea.

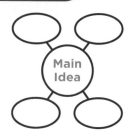

A Main Idea Web can help you find a main idea and supporting details.

Find the main idea of the passage. Then find details that support or explain the main idea.

Saving Trees

Long ago, loggers wanted to cut down huge numbers of trees. Since trees kept getting cut, people became concerned. That led to big disputes and less peace.

"We must protect the trees!" yelled some people. "They are like gems."

"We need trees to make things like pencils!" others yelled back. "Ripened fruit comes from trees and trees give us shade."

Today we have rules to protect some trees. Trees need to be cut, but not so many of them. This way we will have trees ages from now.

Make a **Main Idea Web** for "Saving Trees." Then use it to help you find the main idea and supporting details in the selection.

Large Trees With Large Jobs

by Jennifer Notarangelo

We value trees like gems because they help us in many ways. They help people, plants, and animals stay alive. We depend on trees for things like homes, note pads, and even paint and pancake mix. Trees and plants also make air fresh and clean so we can breathe it. Many trees grow in huge forests. We must take care of forests and keep them clean and safe.

A lot of foods grow in rain forests, including: pineapples, cocoa beans, coconuts, and even the main part of bubble gum!

Rain forests exist in hot places. You might need to take a long trip to visit a rain forest. But things that take place in a rain forest affect each of us. Right now, more species, or kinds, of plants grow in rain forests than in any other place on the planet. Many medicines are made by using plants that only ripen in rain forests.

Bringing Down Trees

Not all people understand that rain forests help each of us. Some want to use the land for other things. They want to cut the trees down. Others want to protect the forests. This leads to big disputes.

Loggers cut trees and sell the wood. As the trees vanish, the land grows bare. Animals must find new homes and food. We need to cut down some trees for people to use, but we must limit how many we take.

Some say that if we keep on cutting trees, rain forests will vanish within the next 100 years.

All this land used to be covered by rain forest. Now it will take many years for the plants and animals to return.

Farmers clear tree stumps and plants and use the land to raise crops. In just a few years, the land is used up and crops cannot grow there. Farmers move on to new land. It takes close to fifty years for the trees and plants to grow back.

Who and What Calls the Rain Forests Home?
Facts about the Rain Forests

Plants	More than 2/3 of the world's plant species are found in the rain forests
Animals	More than 1/2 of the world's animals make their home in the rain forests
People	There are 50 million people who live in the world's rain forests

Trucks are needed to take away the biggest trees. Birds and animals that lived in these trees must find new homes.

In a rain forest, trees have thick stems and big, flat leaves. Trees make shade to protect smaller plants from the sun. Without the trees, the hot sun dries out the land. In time, plants and animals die if there is not enough water.

People are concerned and worried that rain forests keep getting cut down. Governments make rules to save them. Students make clubs. Kids plan to raise money to buy land. Then trees cannot be cut down in that space.

Protect the Forests

Pine forests must be protected as well. Pine trees grow in colder places of the world. It does not rain as much there, so trees must keep each drop of water they get. The trees have figured out a way to do just that.

A leaf on a pine tree is shaped like a needle. Each leaf has a waxy coating that helps it trap water inside. This way, when there is no rain for a long time, the trees have some stored up.

Pine trees are the earliest seed plants that still exist today. That makes these trees more than 300 million years old.

Elk began to disappear as their forest homes vanished. But now laws protect the elks' homes.

The weather is different in a pine forest, just like the animals. You might catch sight of skunks, deer, mice, and elk. In the rain forest you might find lizards, apes, and parrots.

Important new finds are being made each day in the forests. Many medicines are made from plants and animals. Scientists have tried to find more of them but plants and animals keep dying. This happens when their homes are cut down. If this keeps happening, we might not get a chance to find new cures.

Some leaves may be able to cure sickness. Scientists rush to find the cures before the rain forests vanish.

Fires can make forests healthy, but they can also be dangerous. When forest workers make a fire like this, they must be very careful to keep it under control.

Plants and animals are at risk when trees get cut down, but pine forests have an added problem. Pine forests can get too thick in places. Then new trees cannot grow in such tight places. Small fires are started to burn away the fallen needles and sticks. These fires also cut back the number of big trees so new life can begin.

Trees are gems that help all things. We must work to try to keep them safe.

Comprehension Check

Summarize

Read "Large Trees With Large Jobs" again. Fill in the Main Idea Web as you read. Use it to help you summarize the selection.

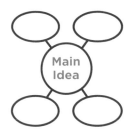

Think About It

1. How are trees helpful to people? Use details from the selection to support your answer.
2. Why do the rain forests need protection?
3. What can we do in school to help save trees? What can we do at home to help save trees?
4. What do you think will happen to the animals that live in the forests if all of their homes are cut down?

Write About It

What might happen if all of the forests are cut down? How might this change our planet? Explain your answer.

Skills and Strategies

Decoding

Decode these words. What do you notice about the spellings?

each	mice	space	witch
page	notch	such	cheer
fetch	chance	match	chest

Vocabulary

relief	dedicated	citizens
advised	succeeded	

Comprehension

MAIN IDEA AND DETAILS The main idea is the most important point of a selection. The details give information that support the main idea.

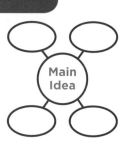

A Main Idea Web can help you find a main idea and supporting details.

Find the main idea of the passage. Then find details that support the main idea.

Fighting for Kids

Long ago, kids did not have the same rights as they do today. Some kids worked long hours each day. Workplaces might be filled with smoke and bad smells. Most kids did not go to school. Dedicated people hatched a plan to change the laws.

"Kids are citizens. Kids need rights," they declared.

They advised kids to choose school instead of work. Their plans succeeded. Today, kids cannot work long hours. Kids have the right to education!

Make a **Main Idea and Details Web**. Then use it to help you find the main idea and details for "Fighting For Kids."

WHICH WAY TO FREEDOM?

BY **LEWIS GARDNER** ILLUSTRATED BY **JAMES E. SEWARD**

CHOOSING TO BE FREE

Being free is a key part of life in the United States. But long ago, life was not free for enslaved people in this country. Enslaved Africans did not have rights as citizens.

A slave family in a cotton field near Savannah, Georgia.

Many men in the South had big homes and a lot of land. Enslaved people helped with hundreds of jobs that needed to be done. Men might use 10 to 100 slaves to plant seeds and gather crops. Slaves also patched fences, dug ditches, and hitched mules to wagons. They stitched clothes, cleaned homes, and baked in kitchens.

Enslaved people helped make slave holders' lives easy and helped make slave holders rich. But slaves did not get paid. And they were not free to leave.

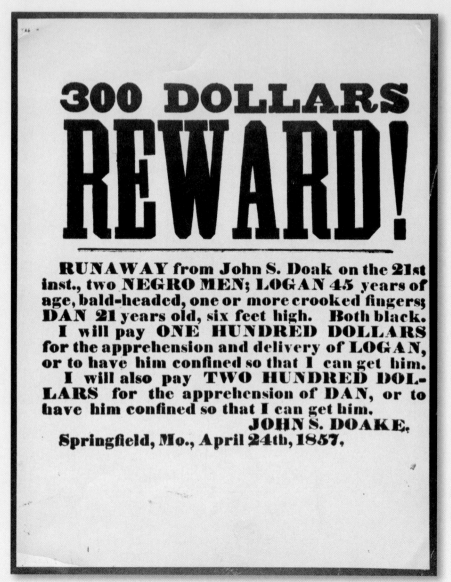

Posters offered rewards for anyone who returned escaped slaves.

Enslaved men, women, and children tried running away. Some succeeded in reaching freedom. To stay free they had to reach a state in the North that did not allow people to be enslaved. Often escaping blacks had to leave behind people they loved.

The trip was long and trying. Most people who were escaping slavery made the trip at night. They hiked in thick woods so they would not be seen. They did not make camps. They did not pass by cities and homes. They tried not to leave traces behind. All of these steps helped to protect them.

Enslaved people had another reason to make the trip at night. Most did not know the path to free states. They used the North Star to lead them the right way.

CHASING A DREAM

The Underground Railroad helped escaped slaves reach the North. It was not a train to ride. It was a band of concerned men and women dedicated to helping people escape from slavery.

Both blacks and whites helped on the Underground Railroad. They felt that it was unfair to enslave people. One man, Levi Coffin, helped at least 3,000 enslaved people escape.

Abolitionist
Levi Coffin
(1798-1877)

The Underground Railroad used codes to discuss plans. The people escaping slavery were called *passengers. Conductors* sneaked them to safe places at night. In daytime, passengers hid in *stations.* A station might be a safe place like a home, a shop, or a church.

Lamps signaled if a site was safe or not. If one lamp was lit, it was safe to stop. Two lit lamps advised a conductor to keep going. They let the conductor see that it was not safe to stop.

Each station had a hiding place. It might be a secret space inside a wall. It might be a hole below the floor. A bed or sofa sometimes hid these secret spots.

Helpers on the Underground Railroad accepted risks that came with the job. They knew they might be sent to jail or even killed. But they were willing to take the risk to help free enslaved blacks.

Hiding places were often hidden in clever spots.

Escaping slaves reached freedom in northern states and Canada by using many different paths.

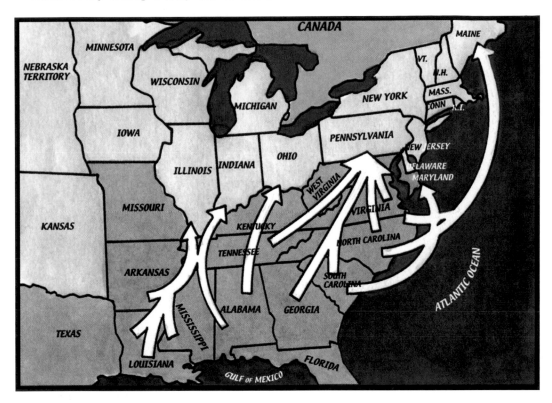

As passengers got closer to free states, they sensed that freedom was within reach. Many could step right into a free state. But others had to cross a big river. Some people swam across, and others waited for a boat to help them finish their journey.

In the North, free blacks felt a mix of fear and relief. The fear was that they might be caught and sent back to slavery. But at least they were free to make new lives. Some bought land, and others had shops to sell things. Being free made them feel happy despite any fear that they might be caught.

Some of the people who escaped slavery wrote tales about their lives. In the tales, they described life as an enslaved person. They wrote about the escape and the trip North. Reading those tales tells us the high price that some enslaved people paid to be free.

Comprehension Check

Summarize

Reread "Which Way to Freedom?". Fill in the Main Idea Web, and then summarize the story.

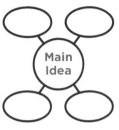

Think About It

1. Why did enslaved people travel at night?
2. How do you think the Underground Railroad got its name?
3. If you were helping enslaved people escape, do you think you would always feel good about what you were doing? Why?
4. How was the life of an enslaved person different from the life of a free person in the North? Explain your answer.

Write About It

In some countries, people are forced to work as punishment for crimes. Do you think this is fair? Explain your answer.

Skills and Strategies

Decoding

Decode these words. What do you notice about the spellings?

roll	goal	catch	old
change	only	moan	reach
banjo	road	throat	omit

Vocabulary

boasted	excitement	refused
costumes	shrieked	fabric

Comprehension

PROBLEM AND SOLUTION In most stories, the characters have a problem. Understanding the problem and how the characters try to solve it helps you understand the story.

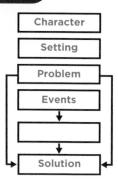

Use your Story Map to help you find the problem and solution.

Identify Tony's problem and the solution.

Finding Tony's Nose

"Where did my nose go?" groaned Tony the clown. Tony was a clown. He could not act without his nose.

"I have a nose!" boasted Mona the juggler. "I can hold a club on mine!"

Tony could hear kids lining up by the road, chatting with excitement. It was nearly time to go!

"Why don't you act without your nose?" asked Lola, a dancer. At first, Tony refused. But the parade must go on! Tony lifted his costume from his trunk.

"Oh!" Tony shrieked. Hiding in the fabric of his costume was his bright red nose!

Make a **Story Map** to help you find the problem and solution in "Finding Tony's Nose."

Joan's First Parade

by Paige Leigh
illustrated by Tyrone Geter

Dancing Down the Roads

Standing in the bright sunlight, Joan swayed from left to right with excitement. The meeting site was filled with people dressed in bright costumes. The band began a fast tune. First Joan heard the quick beat of drums. Then banjos mixed in. Next, dancers strolled toward the band, and singers added a tune.

The parade was set to begin in a little while. Joan had dreamed about this for a long time. The parade went on only once each year in Trinidad. Until this year, Joan's dad had refused to let her take part. But this year she was ready.

"I can't wait!" Joan cried. "I am nine years old. I can jump up and kick my legs at the same time," she noted.

"Being the right age isn't all it takes to be in the parade. Let me share a secret," Mr. Loman advised in a soft and concerned tone. "A parade dancer has a difficult job. It doesn't matter if you are hot, tired, or thirsty. You must keep dancing!"

Joan was excited, but she was also frightened. Her throat felt like it was in a tight knot. Could she dance the whole time? Would her feet keep the beat when her body got tired? The parade would go past each street in the city. The golden sun would be high in the sky before the dancers stopped.

Joan watched the actors and dancers who were the life of the parade. They were so dedicated and full of pride. Joan noticed some drum players that had been in the last parade that Joan had seen. Then there was the man who wore a white mask with horns on each side. People clapped for the wild things he did.

Joan spotted her dad in the packed group. Mr. Loman was the Rag Man. He was a favorite each year. The Rag Man dressed in a costume made with bright strips of fabric. Along the way, the Rag Man made silly faces. He danced in a funny way that made each of us laugh and cheer.

Joan Tries to Meet Her Goal

"It's time! It's time!" a man yelled, running to the front of the line.

It was what Joan and the others had been waiting to hear. The actors in costumes got in line. Next came the band. Last, the dancers stepped into their spots in line. Joan got in place with them. As the drum roll began, she took a deep breath. The parade moved by the bright cones lining the road.

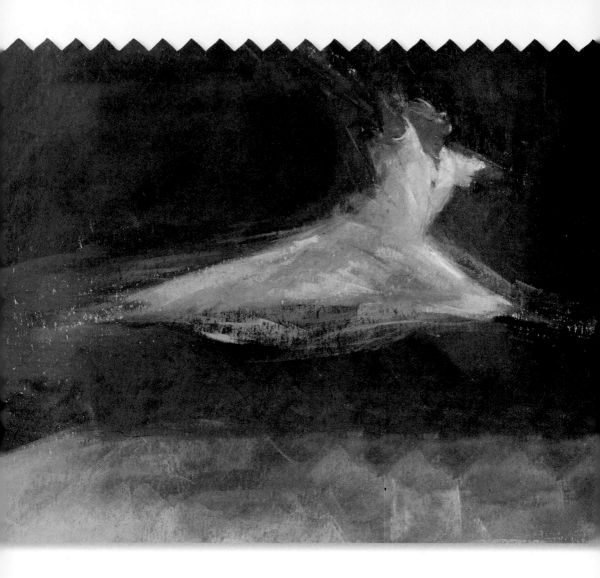

The tunes got louder as the parade neared the core of the city. People came out of their homes and lined the streets to see. Joan stepped to the beat and smiled. She did her best to jump the highest and spin the fastest of all the dancers. She made mistakes, and she got tired, but she didn't stop.

The parade stopped a lot on the way. Each time the actors did a lot of funny things. A girl in a blue hat pretended to bump into a dancer. Another girl made funny faces at a tiny child. The child shrieked and then giggled.

The tunes faded. The parade ended. The tired actors, singers, and dancers sat and rested. Joan felt tired, but she was glad she had succeeded in her goal. She could still hear the music in her mind. Joan tapped her feet and swayed.

"Joan, aren't you tired?" Mr. Loman asked.

With a grin, Joan leaped high up in the air. "Let me share a secret, Dad," she boasted. "I'm a parade dancer. Whether I'm hot, tired, or thirsty, I keep dancing!"

Comprehension Check

Summarize

Read "Joan's First Parade" again.
Fill in the Story Map. Then
summarize the story.

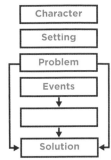

Think About It

1. Why was Mr. Loman worried
   about Joan dancing in the parade?
   What did he say that lets you know?
2. Do you think Joan was sure of herself?
   Support your answer.
3. How would you have felt if you were going to
   be in a parade, like Joan, for the first time?
4. Think about how Joan felt at the beginning of
   the story. How did her feelings change?

Write About It

Why is it important for people to celebrate their
traditions and customs? Explain your answer.

Skills and Strategies

Decoding

Decode these words. What do you notice about the spellings?

sound	count	roam	town
sold	plow	loud	coast
outline	crowd	cowboy	ground

Vocabulary

prowling	daring	well-rounded
swiftly	roaming	

Comprehension

MAKE INFERENCES Making inferences means that you use what you know to help you understand something that is not stated in a story. Making inferences helps you understand what you read.

Text Clues	What You Know	Inferences

To help you make inferences use an Inferences Chart.

Make inferences about the life
Doc Holliday chose.

Doc Holliday

Doc Holliday was a proud cowboy with a swift temper. He prowled from town to town, fighting when he got upset.

Doc had not always been like that. A well-rounded man, Doc had been a dentist before he became a cowboy. Then a doctor told Doc that he was sick, and did not have long to live. Doc became daring. He roamed around the West and pretended he was mean. A man named Wyatt became his pal.

Doc lived for fifteen years after he found out he was sick. He died in peace in his sleep.

Make an **Inferences Chart** for "Doc Holliday." Use it to make inferences about the selection.

A Cowboy's Life

by W. C. Winston

Let's Scout Out the Cowhands

Most people think that the life of a cowboy or cowgirl was filled with excitement. But life was difficult for these dedicated men and women in the Old West.

There weren't fences on the plains. Cows roamed freely. Cowhands had to take care of a herd of cows. If a cowhand did a bad job, cows might get lost. Lost cows could be attacked by prowling wolves.

Most cowhands only made one trip. After that, they would go home and find a different job.

Countless tales boast of brave cowhands like Oliver Loving. He was one of the first men to drive cattle from Texas to the northern United States. It was a daring plan. He went slowly across four states. Loving's trip was a huge success. He sold the cows for a large amount of gold.

Lucille Mulhall was a famed cowgirl. She had been raised on a ranch. A well-rounded lady, she trained horses and roped cows. She proudly roped cows faster than most other people could.

She began roping in shows around the states in the West. Crowds liked to watch Mulhall and her trick pony. Her trick pony could take off a man's coat and then put it back on him!

Nat Love was a well-known cowhand. He led cattle drives for more than 20 years. He roped cows swiftly and rode a horse well. Nat liked a cowhand's life. He liked roaming from place to place. He didn't like staying in crowded towns.

Nat grew up during the Civil War. When he and his family were set free, he left home to become a cowhand.

Nat Love, A Cowhand

Nat was born into slavery. As a kid, Nat spent hours working on the slave holder's land. He helped grow crops and care for the horses and cows. The skills he learned helped him later in life.

When slavery ended, Nat found a job out West. Nat knew how to ride horses and care for cows, so he became a cowhand.

Nat got a prize for his roping skills. He roped cows very fast!

Nat watched other cowboys to see how to rope. They swung a rope up high. Then they had to toss it over a cow's head.

Nat trained and trained to get better at roping. Then he found a job as a trail driver. He got paid thirty dollars each month. That isn't a lot now, but it was then!

When cowhands stopped to rest, the cook prepared big meals for them. The cowhands knew that the cook deserved respect.

Driving cattle was a difficult job, but Nat liked it. He drove 2,000 cows at a time across the plains. Some trips could take three months.

During a three-month trip, cowhands like Nat rode in all kinds of weather. They might have spent more than half a day sitting on a horse. And cowhands slept outside on the ground in a blanket.

If cowboys feared that lightning was nearing, they would sing songs. The singing seemed to relax the cows and stop them from beginning a stampede.

Cows got scared if there was a loud noise or a flash of light in the clouds. It could cause the cows to stampede. Cowhands had to jump on their horses and round up the cows. Love helped get the cows quiet and get them back in place.

Later, trains transported cows from one place to another.

As more and more railroads were made, cowhands were needed less and less. Cows got loaded on trains and shipped north. Nat needed to find a new job. He didn't want to stand behind a plow. He liked to roam the land, so he got a job on a train. A train job allowed Nat to keep traveling.

Today when we think of cowboys and cowgirls, we think of a fun and exciting life. But those men and women worked hard. They became legends of the Old West.

Comprehension Check

Summarize

Read "A Cowboy's Life" again. Then summarize the story.

Think About It

1. Why do you think the first cattle drive was a daring plan? Fill in the Inferences Chart to help you answer.

Text Clues	What You Know	Inferences

2. Why did Nat teach himself how to rope?
3. Do you think you would have liked the life of a cowhand? Why or why not?
4. Reread "Which Way to Freedom?" on pages 94-97. How was Nat's trip across the states the same as or different from the enslaved people?

Write About It

If you wanted to work with animals, what kinds of jobs could you get? Would you like any of those jobs? Explain your answer.

Skills and Strategies

Decoding

Decode these words. What do you notice about the spellings?

moon	fool	noon	food
scout	roof	scoop	goose
crown	troop	cool	cloud

Vocabulary

patriots	country	sign
idea	swooped	

Comprehension

DRAW CONCLUSIONS Authors don't always tell everything that happens. You have to use what you know and what the author does tell you to draw conclusions. Look for clues that support your conclusion.

Text Clues	Conclusion

A Conclusions Chart can help you find clues that support your conclusions.

Draw conclusions from the passage.

Patriot of the Sea

John Paul Jones was a patriot. He sailed a ship and used it to fight the country of England.

Soon, he began fighting with a British ship. The British ship tried to shoot Jones' flag. It was a sign they wanted a fight!

Jones' men were not fools. They became scared of the British troops.

Jones had an idea. "I have not yet begun to fight!" he shouted.

The plan was to swoop down on the British and attack. They did just that and Jones became a hero.

Make a **Conclusions Chart**. Use it to draw conclusions about "Patriot of the Sea."

A Ride in the Moonlight

by Luke Jordan
illustrated by Chris Peterson

Fooling the British

Before the United States was its own country, it was led by the British. The British made a lot of rules that people had to follow. The British kept troops in America to catch people who did not follow British rules.

One rule told Americans they could only get tea at British stores. They also placed a tax on the tea. Tea was a well-liked drink, but Americans did not want to pay high prices and taxes!

A lot of Americans were unhappy. They felt that the British did not treat them in a fair way. Late one night, a bunch of men dressed up as Native Americans to fool the British. The men prowled on to a ship that had tea on it. They scooped up the tea and pitched whole chests of it in Boston Harbor. They hoped to show the British that they did not like the rules.

A lot of men wanted to be free of these British rules. These men were called patriots. The British did not like the patriots.

Paul Revere was a patriot. Following the "Tea Party," he found out about a British plan. Troops had been sent out to Lexington and Concord, two towns outside Boston. A lot of patriots had homes in each place. Paul needed to tell them that the British were on the way.

Paul didn't know if the troops planned to come by land or by sea. Then he had an idea. He asked a patriot to be a lookout for British troops. He would send Paul a hint from Old North Church.

"Light one lamp if British troops go by land," he spoke. "Light two lamps if troops go by sea. I'll watch the church tower's roof for a sign."

Paul told his patriot friend Will about the British plan. Will was dedicated to reaching the patriots, so they hatched a plan. The men would wait to see the lamps in the church. Then each man would ride on a different path toward Lexington. If one man got trapped, the other would still get to the patriots.

It was a cool night. Paul went across the harbor in a boat. Will waited by the church. Then each man saw two lamps in the tower. The British had decided to go by sea! Paul and Will both rode swiftly toward Lexington.

British Troops on the Way

Paul reached Lexington before Will. He shouted to wake up the town. He hitched his horse loosely to a tree. Then he rapped on Sam Adams' door. Sam was a patriot, too.

"Wake up! The British are coming soon. They're hunting for patriots!" Paul yelled. "Get set to fight!"

Will got there soon after Paul. The men went on to Concord to tell the other patriots.

"The British wish to take the hidden arms in Concord. We must go fast," shouted Paul.

British troops saw Paul on the path to Concord. The troops swooped on Paul and grabbed his horse.

Will did not ride close by, so the troops didn't catch him. He rode on a different path to reach Concord.

"You're Paul Revere!" shrieked a soldier. "We were hunting for you. We will take you back to Lexington with us. Then we will chase down the other patriots and take them too. You are not choosing to follow British rules!"

In a daring move Paul told them, "We don't like British rules. We wish to have our own country. Soon we will fight to win our freedom." The troops had a hunch that Paul was telling the truth. They had to tell the other troops to get set for a big fight. They let Paul go but kept his horse so he couldn't reach more patriots.

In Lexington, the patriots waited for the British troops. When they came, the first fight between the troops and the patriots began. After that fight, the patriots united to fight British rule together.

The fight to be free was long and hard. After five years, the patriots reached their goal. They were free from British rule and saw the downfall of the British troops. They made a new country, the United States of America.

Since Paul Revere's ride, a lot of patriotic people have helped keep the United States safe. They defend the right to be free in many places in the world. Maybe some day, people everywhere will have a right to be free.

Comprehension Check

Summarize

Read "A Ride in the Moonlight" again. Then summarize the story.

Think About It

1. Why did Paul Revere want to warn the patriots? Use the Conclusions Chart to help you.

Text Clues	Conclusion

2. Why did Paul become a patriot?
3. What is something you think is important enough to fight for? Why?
4. Fighting is not always the best option. What else could the patriots have done to get freedom?

Write About It

Paul and the other patriots risked their lives to gain freedom. What kinds of freedom do people in the United States have today?

Skills and Strategies

Decoding

Decode these words. What do you notice about the spellings?

part	hard	card	noon
sharp	army	mood	arch
march	bamboo	artist	large

Vocabulary

regarding	offended	grant
delay	committee	basis

Comprehension

FACT AND OPINION A fact is a statement that you can prove to be true. An opinion is the way someone feels or thinks about something so it cannot be proven.

Fact	Opinion

As you read, look for which statements can be proven (facts) and which are somebody's feeling or beliefs (opinions). Use the Fact and Opinion Chart to help you find facts and opinions in the selection

Identify the facts and opinions in the passage.

Standing Up for Their Rights

Long ago, men and women were treated differently regarding voting rights. Women were offended because they wished to take part in voting.

"Grant us rights," they said. "We want to vote just like men."

WOMEN'S
SUFFERAGE
OUR SONS
CAN VOTE
BUT WE
CAN'T

Without **delay,** they decided that this problem had to be fixed. They started committees. Women marched to get voting rights. The right to vote became the basis of the most important movement in history.

Make a **Fact and Opinion Chart** for "Standing Up for Their Rights." Use it to help you find the facts and opinions in the selection.

Susan B. Anthony
Making Her Mark on the Women's Rights Movement

by Luke Jordan

illustrated by Chris Peterson

A Smart Start

A hundred years ago, women in the United States did not have many rights. Women could not own land. If a lady wished to work, there were not a lot of jobs she could get. Even, the pay she got did not belong to her, as it would today.

In a country that took pride in freedom, women had limited rights. One important right that women did not have was the right to vote.

Many women felt that the laws were not fair. They thought that women should have the same rights as men. These women wished to get these rights without delay. They did not want to wait any longer. They decided that they needed to speak out about why the laws were not fair.

They also wanted to explain why women must be considered equal to men. This became the basis for the women's rights movement.

The ladies held meetings to share ideas. Some ladies made speeches and asked others to help them change the laws. Some people liked their plan and wished to be on a committee to help. Other people were offended by what these ladies wanted. The struggle for women's rights had started.

One woman became well known for her part in the women's rights movement. Her name was Susan B. Anthony. She spent more than sixty years trying to change the laws.

Susan gave speeches in front of large crowds. She marched in parades in states all over the country. She did a great deal of work. She hoped that the United States would grant women the same rights that men had.

Susan came from a family that felt that each person must have the same rights. Her family believed that girls should go to school. So Susan learned to read, write, and do math. She worked in her family's shop, too. She saw how her dad treated each worker fairly.

Susan became a teacher at age sixteen. She found out that male teachers got paid much more than female teachers—five times more! Susan was alarmed. She felt it was unfair since both did the same work each day. This is when she began to speak out regarding the lack of equal treatment for females.

An Argument for Equality

Susan felt that enslaved people deserved rights too. She met many people who agreed. They got together to fight for added rights for both enslaved people and ladies.

Susan visited places all over the United States, marching and giving speeches. The public had to buy a ticket to hear her speak. She also helped print a newspaper that she sold. She used the cash she made to help the movement.

Ideas about women's rights reached across the whole country. Men and women began to take action. A man who helped the movement was William Bright. He had been an important man in the army before he went out West to live.

Bright saw that a lot of women in the West worked as hard as men. He felt that women must get the same rights as men. Bright spoke with those who made the laws out West. He asked them to give women the right to vote, too. A lot of men felt that plan made sense. So out West, women were granted the right to vote.

Later, the United States passed a law that gave black men the right to vote. The law said that all *citizens* could vote. In a daring test, Susan tried to vote for a president. She was braver than most women. But she felt that it was her right as a citizen.

The next week, Susan got arrested and went to court. The judge said that she had broken the law and had to pay a fine. Susan explained that she was a citizen *and* a woman. She said she had not broken the law. In the end, Susan did not go to jail or pay a fine. But women still did not have the right to vote!

SUSAN B. ANTHONY

Susan B. Anthony died in 1906. She did not live to see women vote. It took fourteen more years, until 1920, for women to be granted the right to vote.

Today Susan is remembered for her work in the women's rights movement. February 15 is Susan B. Anthony Day. The United States Mint made a dollar coin with her face on it, and two stamps have been printed in her honor.

Comprehension Check

Summarize

Reread "Susan B. Anthony: Making Her Mark on the Women's Rights Movement." Then summarize the story.

Think About It

1. What opinion did William Bright and Susan B. Anthony share? What facts did they base their opinions on? Fill in the Fact and Opinion Chart to help you.

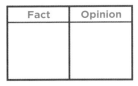

Fact	Opinion

2. Why do you think it took so long for the government to pass a law letting women vote?
3. How would you feel if you had no rights. Why?
4. What do you think students in school should be able to vote on? Why?

Write About It

Why is it important that all people vote during elections? Explain your answer.

Skills and Strategies

Decoding

Decode these words. What do you notice about the spellings?

yard	start	more	form
force	forest	north	party
store	wore	sort	horn

Vocabulary

declared	lantern	fortunately
fragile	exposed	

Comprehension

FACT AND OPINION A fact is a statement that you can prove to be true. An opinion is a belief or thought that cannot be proven.

Fact	Opinion

As you read, look for facts and opinions. Use your Fact and Opinion Chart to help you. Find facts and opinions in the selection.

Identify the facts and opinions in the passage.

Camping at Yellowstone

Yellowstone National Park is the best park. It has trees and hot springs. It was the first forest to be declared a national park.

If you plan to visit Yellowstone at night, do not forget a tent and a lantern. Without a tent, you might expose yourself to wind and rain. A lantern might be fragile, but it will light up dark places in the forest. Lanterns are pretty at night.

A long time ago, people tried to cut down forests. Fortunately, laws were passed to force loggers to stop cutting trees. Now, we can enjoy parks more than ever before!

Make a **Fact and Opinion Chart** for "Camping at Yellowstone." Use it to help you find the facts and opinions in the passage.

A Place for Us to Breathe

by John Turner

illustrated by David Rankin

Trees for You and Me

Pack up your tent and sleeping bag. Don't forget the camp stove and lantern. It's time to go camping in a forest!

Forests are popular places for campers to visit. At night, campers can pitch tents and sleep beneath tall trees. During the day, they can hike on forest paths. Often, hikers can hear birds singing. They can see wild animals such as deer, foxes, or black bears.

152

There was a time when people were not careful about protecting forests. Forest fires burned down many trees. Logging companies also cut down numbers of trees. They used the wood for building things like houses and ships. They also cut trees down to make space for farms and towns. Most logging companies did not plant trees in place of the old ones. So trees in forests began to get used up.

Trees affect all living things, so it is important to defend them. They make air that we can breathe. They make safe homes for animals. Tree branches and leaves provide shade, and tree roots keep soil from washing away. Even trees that die decompose and become food for insects! If we cut down too many trees, animals will lose their homes. The land will be left exposed.

We use trees each day. The paper inside this book was made from a tree. Your desk may be made of wood, too. It's okay if we use some trees to make things that we need. It's also important that we plant new trees to replace the ones that were cut down.

In the past, people were not pleased that loggers cut so many trees. They saw logging companies as thieves who stole trees and gave nothing back in return. These people wanted loggers to stop cutting down so. They also demanded that loggers replant trees for those that were cut down.

These people decided to share their views with the world. Some wrote to newspapers. Others gave speeches explaining why logging is bad for the land. The force of these people got some loggers to stop cutting down so many trees.

National Parks like Yellowstone help us to keep the air clean and the land beautiful.

Who Will Save the Forests?

Others have shown love for the trees, as well. More than two hundred years ago, an artist visited a special site. He made sketches of it. The sketch had trees, big hills, and streams. President Grant thought it looked so nice that he declared it the first national park. President Grant made it against the law to decrease the number of trees in that area. Before this, trees could be harmed or even cut down. With this law, Grant made sure they would be protected. The park was called Yellowstone National Park. Later presidents followed Grant's example and made more places in this country into national parks.

Many "tunnel trees" were cut more than 150 years ago. You can still drive through some of them today.

Each park needed paths for visitors to walk and drive on. But park workers did not want to cut down trees to make the paths. Some park workers had an idea. They cut a wide hole through the biggest trees. Then cars could drive right through them! Park workers thought that cutting the trees would not hurt them. They later found out that was not true. Cutting holes through the trees was unhealthy for them. Now paths only go around trees.

Lightning can blast a tree apart. The tree may die even if it has been left standing, because it wil not be able to protect itself.

Park laws keep the forests safe from logging. But they can't keep forests safe from forest fires. Lightning can start fires and flames can race swiftly through the forest. Most trees have thick bark that keeps them safe. But fires can burn right through some trees. Then only the strongest trees stay alive.

For years, park workers thought that all fires hurt forests. Today we know that some fires can be good. Fires clear out weak trees and leave room for bigger trees to grow. Park workers try to do the same thing. They set small fires, but they are careful to control where the fires burn. These fires help the forest just like fires started by lightning do. They clear out fragile trees and leave space for strong trees to grow.

Fortunately, people worked very hard to save trees. They knew that keeping our forests safe was important. Land was turned into national parks. These parks are protected for all people, both now and in the future.

On your next camping trip, take a look around and enjoy the pretty sights. Then give thanks to all those ordinary people who worked hard to make national parks possible.

Comprehension Check

Summarize

Reread "A Place for Us to Breathe." Then summarize the story.

Think About It

1. Are forest fires more harmful or helpful? Use the Fact and Opinion Chart to help you.

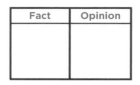

Fact	Opinion

2. Why do we need to protect our national parks?

3. If you lived near a forest where a logging company wanted to cut down trees, how would you react? Why?

4. Reread "Susan B. Anthony: Making Her Mark on the Women's Rights Movement" on pages 145-146. How was that fight different from the people who stopped loggers? Explain.

Write About It

What did we learn about how people struggled to save forests? How can we continue to keep our environment safe?

Skills and Strategies

Decoding

Decode these words. What do you notice about the spellings?

stir	enter	bird	shirt
nurse	corner	desert	burn
order	orbit	urge	perk

Vocabulary

images	remarkable	echoes
fret	unique	

Comprehension

COMPARE AND CONTRAST

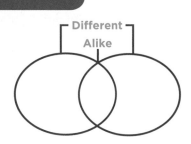

When you compare two things, you see how they are alike. When you contrast, you see how they are different.

Analyzing what happens in a story allows you to notice similarities and differences between characters, events, and settings.

To help you compare and contrast things in the story use your Venn Diagram.

What did Ernie expect to find and what did he actually find?

WHAT WILL TURN UP?

"Sift the dirt like this," Miss Fern said, pushing the soil by her knees. "Old things lay hidden beneath this dirt."

Images passed through Ernie's mind. He saw himself holding a remarkable find. He saw Miss Fern praising him, calling him clever and smart. The words echoed through his mind.

After his daydream ended, he fretted. Would he find something neat? Minutes later, he tugged out a small, pointed rock. He turned to show Steve.

"We both found unique arrowheads!" said Steve.

Make a **Venn Diagram** for "What Will Turn Up?" Use it to figure out how things are alike and how they are different.

A DESERT VACATION

by Mary Ramirez
illustrated by Shelly Hehenberger

A BURNING HOT TRIP

Kurt dribbled under the hoop. "Star hoops player, Kurt 'Slam Dunk' Birch runs fast," Kurt cheered. "It's an impossible shot! Birch Jumps! He shoots! He scores! Amazing!"

"Come on in, Kurt!" Kurt's mom called from the back porch. Kurt did not want to go inside. He knew that his mom was going to make him pack for his trip.

Kurt was going to visit his pal Asher. Asher's family had moved from Southern California to the desert last year. Kurt missed Asher, but he knew he would not like the burning hot desert.

Kurt wanted to have fun. But he knew there would be no beach for swimming and no hills for hiking. It would also be too hot to play ball.

Kurt heard his name as soon as he stepped off the plane.

"Hi, Kurt!" yelled Asher.

"Hi, Asher. I hope I don't burn up from being exposed to the hot sun out here!"

"Don't fret," said Asher's dad as they left the airport and walked to the truck. "You can swim at the local pool."

"I hope I don't pass out from heatsroke," Kurt wrote to his mom on a postcard. Then he looked out the window. The sun was setting behind a huge cliff.

Kurt saw many remarkable rocks in the distant cliffs. The sun lit up the rocks, and Kurt could see a hundred shades of red. Black shadows seemed to split the rocks in places.

"Rain, wind, and time made those shapes," declared Asher. "It took many years and plenty of rain."

Asher's sister, Fern, came over to the truck as they pulled in the driveway. "You guys took the detour. It's better than TV, isn't it?" She asked, smiling.

Kurt kept looking at the cliffs in the sunset. He smiled. "The rocks look so neat. I've never seen anything that color."

"The rocks look red in the sunset," said Fern. "But in the day they are all shades of tan, brown, gray, and pink."

"The rocks make echoes, too," added Asher. "If you yell, you can hear the rocks yell back."

That night, Fern gave Kurt a pile of postcards. On the back of each card there were notes about the photo. Kurt and Asher looked at the postcards. Kurt liked a postcard of a glowing white flower. This flower was unique because it could grow in the desert.

Kurt stared at a card of a wooden doll. It had horns and a beak. The card said Native Americans believed that spirits living in the dolls protected and helped them. Some dolls were made for kids to remind them to be upright in their actions.

A POWERFUL SITE

Kurt and Asher looked at heaps of postcards with Native American images on them. Soon they came to a postcard with baskets on it. Native Americans had woven the baskets out of grasses. They had used them to carry food and water.

Then Asher said, "Tomorrow we're going to go see the real stone buildings that the Hisatsinom (ee•SAH•tse•nom) built. Maybe we will also see the baskets or the dolls on our trip."

Kurt smiled. "That would be great!" Maybe the desert wasn't such a bad place after all.

In the morning, Kurt and Asher were excited to get going. The whole family got in the truck, and Asher's dad pointed to a cliff far away. "That's where we're going today," he grinned.

A guide met them at the top of the cliff. He told them about the people who made homes in the cliffs many years back. They used the land for farming. They got water for the crops from digging under the land. The people were very capable.

The guide told how the people made clay pots and grass baskets. Then he spoke about spirit dolls. Kurt had not forgotten the notes on the postcards. "Men dressed as spirits and danced in the town," explained the guide. "Then men gave dolls to the kids to remind them to listen."

"My Mom would love a doll like that!" said Kurt. Asher smiled.

As they got back in the truck, Kurt saw a doll in a store window.

"Wait!" Kurt said. He ran into the store and paid for the doll.

Kurt smiled and went outside. "Mom will like it," he said. "I am glad she told me to visit Asher in the desert. It was fun!" he smiled, "and maybe the doll will help me remember how much I liked the desert!"

Comprehension Check

Summarize

Read "A Desert Vacation" again. Then summarize the story.

Think About It

1. How was life in the desert different from life where Kurt lives? Use details from the story to fill in your chart.

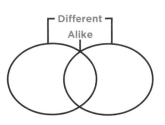

2. Why didn't Kurt want to go to the desert?
3. Would you enjoy living in the desert? Why or why not?
4. What things made Kurt change his mind about the desert? Use details from the selection in your answer.

Write About It

Kurt didn't want to go to the desert because he thought he wouldn't like it. After he went, Kurt realized he did like the desert. What can you learn from Kurt's experience? Explain.

Skills and Strategies

Decoding

Decode these words. What do you notice about the spellings?

wrung	knob	wrong	climb
knelt	plumber	lamb	knock
knit	thumb	wrist	wrap

Vocabulary

knoll	wreck	grave
variety	combing	seized

Comprehension

DRAW CONCLUSIONS

Sometimes the author leaves something for readers to figure out.

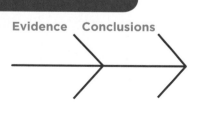

When that happens, readers must draw their own conclusions.

A Conclusions Diagram can help you organize the facts and details the author states directly. By using these facts and details as evidence, you can draw a conclusion.

What can you tell about Tony?

Tony the Pilot

"Tony," called the spaceship pilot. "I hurt my wrist last night, and I need to take some medicine. Will you take over for a bit?"

Tony was the newest man on the spaceship. He knew how to take off, how to fly to a planet, and how to land. Once, he had even landed on a high knoll. But, he had never flown a spaceship by himself. He didn't want to wreck it.

"Okay," said Tony, biting his thumbnail gravely. He stared at the variety of buttons and combed his pockets for his key. Then he seized the steering wheel. No one was sitting beside him. After a few minutes Tony felt fine!

Make a **Conclusions Diagram**. Use the evidence in "Tony the Pilot" to help you draw conclusions.

Hope's Trip to Planet Wren

by Mark Allen
illustrated by Karel Hayes

Combing for Rocks

The students sat and whispered as Mr. Knorr spoke. They were excited for the trip to finally happen. The lift-off had been smooth, and Earth now looked like a tiny dot below. The class would spend the night on the spaceship. They would land early the next morning on Planet Wren.

"Tomorrow morning we will be exploring Crumb Hill," explained Mr. Knorr. "It's a big knoll on Planet Wren that has a variety of unique rocks."

"A scientist named Dr. Wright asked that we take pictures of the rocks and measure them," said Mr. Knorr. "Dr. Wright also asked that each student bring back a rock for her to look at. Now get some rest. We will land on Planet Wren early tomorrow morning!"

Hope knew that bringing back a rock was very important. Dr. Wright studied rocks. Hope wanted hers to be the most desirable one.

Hope had a hard time sleeping that night. She tried writing in her journal until at last she fell asleep.

"We've got ten minutes left before we land!" called Mr. Knorr the next morning. "Everybody up and into your spacesuits!"

The kids put on silver spacesuits and waited. After the spaceship docked, the kids climbed out and ran down the ramp to the space station.

"Don't forget to look around and find a special rock for Dr. Wright!" Mr. Knorr shouted after them.

Hope worked with her pal, Ralph, on Crumb Hill.
Hope was responsible for taking pictures of the
rocks. Ralph knelt down and measured the rocks.

The kids worked for an hour and then had lunch.
After lunch, they went back to take more pictures
and to to find collectible rocks. Hope was getting
tired by the time Mr. Knorr gathered them together
to board the spaceship.

"Here's the rock that I am taking back!" Ralph yelled. He held up a bright green rock between his index finger and his thumb. It lit up when he squeezed it. "Isn't it remarkable?"

"Oh no! I've forgotten to pick a rock!" Hope thought. She looked around and seized a rock sitting near her ankle. It was ugly, brown, and coated in dirt. Hope frowned and stuck it in her pocket.

The spaceship left Planet Wren. Each kid held up his or her rock to show Mr. Knorr. The phone in the cabin rang, and Mr. Knorr picked it up. He listened and wrinkled his forehead. When he hung up, he had a serious look on his face.

"That was our pilot, Kelly," Mr. Knorr announced. "She says there's a small problem with our spaceship and she's stopping to fix it. But don't fret, class. We will be out of here in no time."

Hope gazed out of the window. She hoped Mr. Knorr was right.

What a Wreck!

"I once read a story about a spaceship that got stuck," Ralph whispered. "It was left sitting in space for a long time before someone came to help."

Hope wrung her hands. She felt numb and had a knot in her belly. She didn't want to stay in space for that long. She wanted to go home.

Mr. Knorr saw her. "Don't worry, Hope," he said. "I'm sure Kelly will fix it soon. Then we'll be on our way back to Earth."

Just then, they heard a knock at the door. Kelly and her team stepped into the cabin. The kids knew something was wrong. "The problem is a bit bigger than we thought," she admitted. "Our battery is dead, so our spaceship can't move. We will have to wait until help arrives."

Suddenly, Kelly pointed at Hope's hand.

"Is that yours?" she asked. She was pointing at the dull brown rock Hope held. "That's an electric rock! We can use it to recharge the battery!" She took the rock and ran out of the cabin.

A few minutes later, the phone rang again. Mr. Knorr picked it up, and his grave look turned into a smile.

"It worked!" he declared. "We're going home."

Hope heard the spaceship rumble as it started up again. She felt happy that the spaceship was fixed, but she felt sad, too. "I can't take my rock back to Dr. Wright anymore," she told Mr. Knorr.

"That's okay," Mr. Knorr said. "You have a neat story to tell her about the electric rock. And who knows? Maybe scientists will even be able to discover a new use for the rock. Good work, Hope!"

Comprehension Check

Summarize

Reread "Hope's Trip to Planet Wren." Then summarize the story.

Think About It

Evidence   Conclusions

1. How did Hope feel about the rock before the spaceship's battery died? After? Use the Conclusions Diagram to help you answer.
2. Why did Hope have a hard time sleeping the night before the spaceship landed?
3. Would you enjoy a trip to space? Why?
4. Reread "A Desert Vacation" on pages 164–165. How did Kurt feel about traveling to a new place? Compare his feelings to Hope's.

Write About It

If humans built a city on a different planet, how would life be different?

Skills and Strategies

Decoding

Decode these words. What do you notice about the spelling?

kneel	enjoy	wrote	toy
voice	comb	soy	coin
point	noise	choice	disappoint

Vocabulary

confidence	offices	accept
assured	confused	

Comprehension

CHARACTER AND SETTING A character is a person or animal in a story. The setting is where and when a story takes place. Knowing the characters and settings of a story can help us understand what happens in the story.

Character	Setting

Use the Character and Setting Chart to help you list important details about characters and settings.

Find the characters and the setting.

My Brave Uncle

My uncle sat down at the old table in the kitchen and folded his arms. His pointed chin was lifted high with confidence.

He said, "I've decided to vote. I will find out who is running for office. Then I will go to the general store and make my choice."

"Can I join you?" I asked. I hoped he'd accept. "Yes, you won't annoy me," he assured me. "Is voting important to you?"

"Of course!" I said. "It's very important to have a voice. I will enjoy voting one day."

Make a **Character and Setting Chart** for "My Brave Uncle." Identify the characters and setting.

Grandpop's Brave Choice

by Richard B. Henry

illustrated by Michael Hobbs

Grandpop Lets His Voice Be Heard

Grandpop marched proudly through town. He had a spring in his step as he walked along the street with confidence. He nodded to the men and raised his hat to the women as he passed. I followed behind him, trying to keep up. Grandpop had waited for me to finish my chores so that I could go with him. Now he was in a hurry. He couldn't be late.

"Today is a special day!" Grandpop kept telling me, with a look of joy on his face. "Today I get to vote!"

Finally, Grandpop stopped outside a big store. A sign hung in the window. It had big red letters on it that spelled out, "Vote Here!" Grandpop's face broke into a smile. He opened the door and walked in.

A man was reading a newspaper behind a desk. He looked up when we entered and walked around his desk toward us. "Hello, Mr. Knox," the man said. "What brings you in today?"

"I came to vote, Mr. Boyd!" Grandpop said in a serious voice. "I know my rights. The government says that I have the right to vote. Today I'm going to do just that!"

Mr. Boyd looked past Grandpop at a large wall clock. "You only have five minutes left before the store closes. You'll have to hurry," he advised.

Grandpop pointed back at the clock with his thumb. "Five minutes is plenty of time," he assured Mr. Boyd.

Mr. Boyd nodded and handed Grandpop a paper with rows of names on it. "This is a ballot," he explained. "There are a variety of offices to vote for. Mark your choice in each row. Then drop your paper into this box."

Grandpop took a pencil out of his coat pocket. He read the names written on the ballot. Then, he carefully made a mark in each row. When he completed it, he smiled and dropped the ballot into the box.

A Big Disappointment

"I've finished voting," Grandpop said proudly. "We can go home now."

As we turned to leave, I saw that a noisy crowd had gathered outside the store. Some people had angry looks on their faces as we passed. I felt scared, but Grandpop seized my hand. He stood straight and tall as we walked outside and through the town.

"I don't understand," I said. "Why were those men looking at us with such mean faces?"

"Some people just can't accept that people are people, no matter what color their skin is," Grandpop said. We walked back home along the dirt road. "When I was a kid, black people didn't have any rights. Many of us were enslaved. I never got to go to school to learn how to read and write like you. Someone had to secretly teach me the alphabet."

"But then there was a big war, right Grandpop?" I asked. I knew about the war from stories that Grandpop had told me.

"That's right," answered Grandpop. "Enslaving others is wrong, so some people went to war to stop it. After the war we were all freed. Now black men enjoy the right to vote."

We stopped to rest in the shade. Suddenly, something Grandpop had said seemed odd. "Only men are allowed to vote?" I asked, confused.

"Yes, only men," answered Grandpop.

"That doesn't seem fair, Grandpop," I said. "Shouldn't everybody be allowed to vote?"

"You're right, my boy," said Grandpop as he took off his hat. "It's not right to keep anyone from voting."

Ferry
departs
at 5:00 pm

We stood up and began to walk again. On the river, a white ferryboat floated slowly towards us. The people joked and chatted loudly, making a lot of noise.

"Boy, I'd sure like to ride in a fancy boat like that," I said.

"It does look like fun," Grandpop agreed. Then he looked disappointed. "That's another way that things aren't fair," he continued. "To ride that boat, I'd have to pay the same fare as a white person. I'd have to sit in a different room, though."

Grandpop sighed. "We'd better hurry so we won't be late for dinner," he said.

When we got home, Grandpop joined my mom and dad in the house. He told them about his interesting day. I sat outside and thought about all that I had heard and seen.

It didn't seem fair that all people didn't have the same rights. A whole war had to be fought for blacks to get some rights. It was wrong that some people couldn't vote because of how they looked. I hoped that one day soon women would have voting rights. Sometimes, when people were granted more rights, other people still didn't like it. Grandpop didn't care what anyone else said, though. He had shown a lot of courage by voting. I sure was proud of him!

Comprehension Check

Summarize

Read "Grandpop's Brave Choice" again. Then summarize the story.

Think About It

1. How is the setting important to this story? Use the Character and Setting Chart to help you.

Character	Setting

2. How did people feel about Mr. Knox voting? How do you know?

3. Do you think you would feel and act the same as Mr. Knox did when he left the store? Why?

4. How did Mr. Knox show courage in this story? Explain.

Write About It

What are peaceful things we can do today to make sure that people have the rights they deserve? Explain your answer.

Skills and Strategies

Decoding

Decode these words. What do you notice about the spellings?

soy	battle	gobble	label
cattle	angel	voyage	tunnel
avoid	rattle	able	soil

Vocabulary

injure	odor	attempts
ordinarily	survive	

Comprehension

AUTHOR'S PURPOSE Authors can have different reasons for writing. An author might be giving information, trying to convince you of something or just telling a story.

Clues	Author's Purpose

An Author's Purpose Chart helps you identify clues to the author's purpose for writing the story.

Identify the author's purpose.

Watch Out for Little Animals

Little animals always have to be ready for battle. If they aren't, they might be injured or gobbled up! When in danger, animals can either run or hide. Some little animals also have other ways to defend themselves.

Some animals have a shell or quills to protect them. Other animals give off a bad odor. Still other animals taste very bad. If an enemy takes a nibble, it won't attempt to again!

Ordinarily, animals do not try to hurt people or other animals. They need these defenses to level their chances of surviving.

Make an **Author's Purpose Chart** for "Watch Out for Little Animals." Use it to figure out why the author wrote the story.

BIG IDEAS FOR LITTLE ANIMALS

by Doris Kerr

Quills, Rattles, and Claws

Some little animals can easily be eaten by bigger animals. If they don't watch out, a bigger animal may seize them and gobble them up!

These weaker animals have different ways to survive. Some have claws, teeth, or other body parts that help them fight back. Some can run quickly so that others cannot catch them. There are even animals that can hide by changing colors. This way they blend in with the things around them.

Some animals have unique tools to keep themselves out of harm's way. A porcupine has a coat of very sharp quills on its back. When it thinks it will be attacked, a porcupine makes clicking noises as a warning. If it still feels scared, it rolls itself into a ball and sticks out its quills.

Even hungry animals will stay away from a quarrel with a ball of pointy quills. Quills are as sharp as needles and can come off the porcupine and stick into its attacker like thorns. That hurts! Then the animal knows not to nibble on any more porcupines.

If this lion gets any closer, those sharp quills may stick in his skin. He had better watch out!

A snake does not use its tongue to defend itself.
Its tongue helps it to smell and feel things around it.

A rattlesnake has fangs and a rattle that keep it safe. If it feels like it is in danger, a rattlesnake can shake its tail. This creates a rattling sound. This rattle acts as a warning to other animals.

If an animal still attempts to injure the snake, the snake can use its fangs to bite. Then it squirts venom through its fangs. This venom can make the other animal stop moving or even kill it.

A skunk will not bite animals that attack it. It has a different way to keep itself safe. When it is afraid, a skunk stamps its feet as a warning. Ordinarily, the skunk does not cause harm. But if it is still scared, it sprays a light yellow liquid that has a very strong odor.

Most animals run from the skunk's spray. Besides the bad smell, the spray can hurt eyes and noses.

A skunk's markings make it easy to spot. A sprayed animal will remember those markings and never attack another skunk.

Running from Battle

Some animals do not use sharp teeth or claws as a way to stay safe. Instead they try to stay away from anything that might eat them.

Rabbits have long, strong hind legs. These legs help them run fast and assure their safety. They can often escape from danger because of their speed. They may quickly crawl down an underground tunnel, too.

A rabbit also has long ears and big eyes. Its ears help it hear sounds that are far away. Its eyes help it see little movements. A rabbit uses its big eyes and ears to catch any sign of danger.

Rabbits can move one ear while keeping the other one still. This helps them find the source of noises.

Monkeys can hold on to branches with their hands, feet, or tail. That helps them climb trees very quickly.

Like rabbits, monkeys run when they're scared. Instead of running on land, a monkey climbs up high into a tree. It has long arms that help it swing from branch to branch with confidence. It climbs until it is safely out of reach. Most other animals cannot climb as well, so the monkey stays safe. Some monkeys can stay in trees for a whole lifetime!

When monkeys get scared, they may use their voices to make a loud, high-pitched screech. This warning tells other monkeys to climb higher. This way they will all stay away from the danger.

This seahorse looks just like coral, so other animals won't be able to find it.

Simple Ways to Hide

A seahorse also hides when it gets scared. It can't swim very fast, so it can't get away. It can swim into a bundle of seaweed and wrap its tail around one piece. This way the seahorse will not float away. It can hide in other places, too.

Seahorses can change the shade of their skin to blend in with the seaweed. That makes it much harder for animals to find them. Other animals think that the seahorses are part of the seaweed.

A walking stick is an insect that is hard for other animals to see. It does not change colors like a seahorse. Instead it stays brown, just like the bark of a tree.

A walking stick is long and skinny, so it looks like a twig or a little branch not a tasty morsel. Flying high, a bird can't tell that the walking stick is really an insect. The bird thinks it's just a bit of wood, so it doesn't eat the walking stick. Since a walking stick is hard for animals to see, it is hard for them to eat, too!

If you were a hungry animal, would you eat this walking stick as a snack? Would you be able to find it at all?

Animals live on land, in the sky, and even underwater. Wherever you go, there will always be interesting animals around you.

Each animal in our world is important. No matter how little each one is, it still has a special role to fill.

If one kind of animal disappears, then animals that eat that kind will begin to disappear, too. The tools that weak animals use to stay safe make it easier for them to stay alive. While some of these animals may still get eaten, others will survive. Our world will then stay full of life for all to enjoy.

Comprehension Check

Summarize

Read "Big Ideas for Little Animals" again. Then summarize the story.

Think About It

1. What message does the author share with the reader? Fill in the Author's Purpose Chart with details from the story to help you.

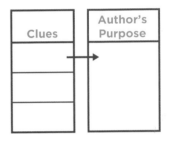

2. Why do many animals warn before they attack?

3. Tell about another animal that has a special way to stay safe.

4. Which is the best way for animals to stay safe: fight back, run away, or hide? Why?

Write About It

Why is it important for animals to be able to protect themselves? Explain your answer.

Skills and Strategies

Decoding

Decode these words. What do you notice about the spellings?

camel	stall	settle	law
crawl	needle	alarm	taught
cause	mall	jaw	hawk

Vocabulary

structure	absolute	foolishly
authored	developed	

Comprehension

MAKE GENERALIZATIONS To make a generalization, use what you know to decide if something is true for a group.

Information from Text	
Prior Knowledge	
Generalization	

A Generalizations Chart helps you make broad statements that describe ideas or events. This will help you monitor your understanding of what you read.

Form generalizations about democracy.

What is Democracy?

The structure of a democracy is very different from a monarchy. A democracy is designed so that each person has part of the power.

In a monarchy, one leader has absolute power. This can be awful if the leader is foolish or mean. The country has to listen anyway.

America was not always a democracy. The British monarchy ruled over the people who lived here. Patriotic men here authored a letter to the king, declaring freedom. This country has developed into a democracy because of those men.

Make a **Generalizations Chart**. Use it to help you make generalizations as you read "What is Democracy?"

☆ A NEW ☆ GOVERNMENT

by Irene Springman

A NEW FORM OF GOVERMENT

The United States has been a country for just over two hundred years. Before that, the states were all royal British colonies. They were called American colonies because they were in North America.

The British made laws that the colonists had to follow. They also charged high taxes. The Americans did not like the laws and felt this treatment was unfair. They wished to make choices for themselves.

People in America began to chat. They wished for a choice and a voice in the government. They wanted to make their own rules.

Lawyers, silversmiths, farmers, and patriots met and developed a model for a new kind of government. The men made a list of the rights for all citizens.

The men signed the paper on July 4, 1776 and sent it to the British royals. The paper declared American freedom from the British. The Americans would no longer be ruled by British laws. The paper became the basis for our government today.

People, such as George Washington, spoke out about how they thought the government would work best.

Washington bravely leads his army across the Delaware River to attack British troops.

The British did not like what they saw. They felt that the Americans were acting foolishly. They sent an army to assure that the Americans followed the British laws. But this attempt was more difficult than the British thought it would be. The Americans were ready to fight battles for a cause: freedom.

The fighting lasted for eight awful years. Nonetheless, the Americans ideas of freedom survived. The United States was born!

Now the Americans had to build the new government. The men worked from the outline they had written before. The government plan called for three parts, or branches. No one branch would get absolute power. The three branches would share the power and check each other. This is still the plan today!

Each branch has a separate job. One branch is run by the President. Another branch is made up of the lawmakers. Judges make up the third and final branch. The citizens have a say in the government, too. We vote for people who we believe can protect us from injustice and injury.

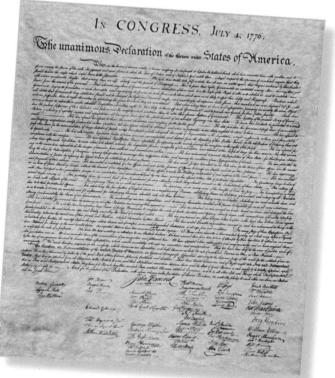

Colonists explained why they wanted to be free from British King George III in the Declaration of Independence.

The Oval Office is where the U.S. President conducts daily business.

IMPORTANT JOBS

The President has a lot of power. The President leads a few different parts of the government. The President suggests laws that help citizens. The President decides if a law, authored by the lawmakers, is passed. The President signs a law if it is right for the citizens. But, the President can choose not to sign a law, too.

The President is also in charge of the armed forces. The armed forces defend our land. The President meets with leaders in other nations to share ideas and solve problems. Together, all of the leaders attempt to make the world safe for everybody.

The lawmakers make up another branch of government. The lawmakers speak for the citizens. They draw up new laws to help the citizens of our country.

First, lawmakers take note of what the citizens say is important. Then they discuss these ideas with other lawmakers. The lawmakers need to make sure the new laws will be helpful. Finally, the whole group votes on a bill, or plan, for a law. If most of the group is in agreement, the bill becomes a law. Then the President can sign it.

The President talks with lawmakers. They work together with citizens, to make laws that will help the country.

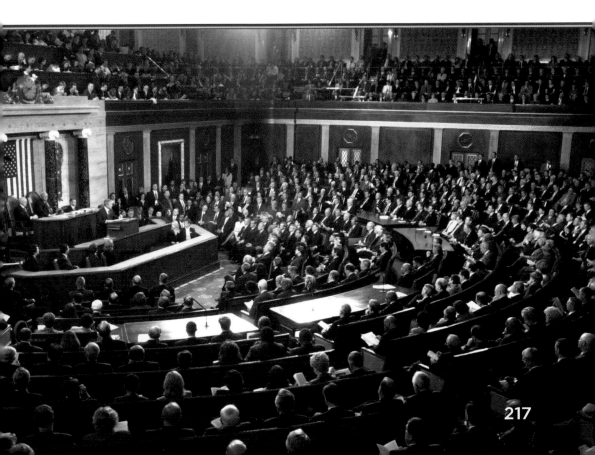

The Supreme Court is made up of nine judges. That way there can never be a tie when they vote.

The third branch is the Supreme Court. The Court is made up of nine judges. The judges' job is to help people understand the laws. They also make sure the laws are fair. They hear cases when people disagree with a law or a decision. Some cases are very hard to understand.

The judges hear the facts from both sides. One side explains how the law is faulty. The other side will try to prove the law is fair. Next, the judges explore the law and the arguments and make a decision. Then the judges vote and make an announcement saying which side is right. Finally, they explain the decision so citizens will understand the laws.

Sometimes judges will change a decision that was made in the past. They see that the world is different now than it was before. There may be new facts that make the old law unfair. So the judges hear another case and may change the law.

At one time a court decided to separate people because of skin color. Over fifty years later the court heard another case about this law. A family wanted all children to be taught the same way. This time the judges made a different choice. They decided people could not be separated based on their skin color.

In 1954 the Supreme Court decided it was unfair to send children to different schools based on the color of their skin.

When we vote, we choose leaders that we think will make the world a better place.

Government structure allows each of the three branches to do its job. But the citizens have an important job, too.

Citizens must follow the laws and voice how they feel about them. Citizens do this by voting.

People get to make a choice for President. They can vote for the lawmakers, too. They even vote for some judges. It can be hard to make a choice. But thanks to our forefathers, we get to make choices!

Comprehension Check

Summarize

Reread "A New Government." Then summarize the selection.

Think About It

1. Why did the Americans want a new government? Use the Generalizations Chart to help you answer.

Information from Text	
Prior Knowledge	
Generalization	

2. Why should judges help people understand laws?

3. Which branch of the government do you think you would like to work for? Why?

4. Reread "Grandpop's Brave Choice" on page 188. Tell why it is important to vote.

Write About It

Is it a good idea to revisit old laws? Why?

Skills and Strategies

Decoding

Decode these words. What do you notice about the spellings?

blow	lawn	load	foam
cause	bold	most	snow
coach	follow	thaw	hotel

Vocabulary

dense	destroyed	treacherous
quarrel	shelter	

Comprehension

DESCRIPTION An author picks words very carefully to paint a picture inside of your head. They use words to make events and characters seem more real.

Signal Words	Descriptive Facts

Use a Description Chart to list details about something in a story. Then write about what each word teaches you about the story.

Find the descriptive words in the passage.

Stuck in the Snow

When the wind blows and rain begins to fall, a big storm can follow. Very cold air can cause the rain to turn into dense snow. Power lines can be destroyed from the weight of the snow! During a snowstorm, roads can become treacherous.

Bright white snow hits the ground. Quiet streets become loud with the howling wind. Some even say that storms can sound like the sky is having a quarrel with itself. In a bad storm, people race to shelters to keep safe.

Make a **Description Chart** for "Stuck in the Snow." Then use it to write about what happens during a storm.

Follow the Weather

by Claire Jackson

Why Does the Wind Blow?

The day begins with a big blue sky. A few fluffy clouds float by us as the sun glows brightly. There is a gentle breeze. It is the perfect day for a picnic.

Later, the wind begins to blow a little harder. Thick clouds approach us and the sky gets dark. Before long—*boom, crackle, crash*! Thunder rumbles and lightning streaks across the sky. It's a thunderstorm! Rain pours down. People run for shelter. The picnic is over!

Weather can develop very quickly. It can be warm and sunny one minute. Then it can be cool and rainy the next minute. What causes the weather to change?

There are layers of gas that cover the whole Earth. These gases make up the atmosphere. The layer that is closest to Earth is made up of air. This air is always moving. Because water and land heat differently, the air above these spots does, too. Air moving over water will get warmer and wetter. Air moving over land will get cooler and drier.

A view of Earth shows how the weather can be different all over the world.

Clouds can be in the sky even on sunny days. It's hard to guess when the weather might change.

Cool air is more dense than warm air. What does this mean? The tiny elements in cold air are closer together than in warm air. Think of cold air as being heavier. Cold air sinks and moves below warm air. In the same way, warm air rises over cool air. The repeated rising and sinking of air makes wind.

Sometimes large masses of air move. The air can be cool or warm. If cool air meets warm air, some big changes can happen. At first, a person might notice a few more clouds in the sky. The air might feel cooler or warmer.

Storm clouds can make the sky so dark that day seems like night.

Sometimes changes can happen quickly. The sky will suddenly fill with dark clouds. Thunder will sound, and lightning will flash in the sky. Most of the time, rain will fall. But sometimes there are other changes.

Strong swirling winds can roll in and the land can flood. Trees can be ripped from the land, and homes can be wrecked. It is as if the sky is having a quarrel with itself. These arguments can become dangerous storms, and people can get hurt.

Weather Can Cause Harm

Thunderstorms are created when cool and warm air meet. Warm, wet air flows upward, cooling and forming into tall dark clouds. The dark clouds are filled with water that falls as rain. Then lightning can spark and heat the air around it. The hot air meets the cool air and makes thunder.

Thunderstorms can be very dangerous. Lightning can strike Earth and cause a fire. It can flow through wires and harm computers and phones. Strong winds can snap tree branches. Finally, heavy rain can cause flooding. But thunderstorms usually last only a short time.

If you see lightning, go inside. Standing in water, in open fields, or by tall objects is dangerous!

Tornadoes are nicknamed "twisters" because they twist and spin.

Sometimes the air in a tall, dark cloud rises very quickly. It pulls warm, wet air up at a very fast speed. The moving air begins to spin. This wind can spin up to three hundred miles per hour. The wind forms a cone shape and dips to the ground. It's a tornado!

No one can predict the movements a tornado will make. A tornado can rip up trees. It can even pick up cars and houses and move them. Most tornadoes last for only a few minutes. But many things in their paths can be destroyed.

How A Tornado Forms

Warm air rising in strong updraft →

Low-pressure spot →

Another kind of treacherous storm happens over warm ocean water. It begins with dark clouds growing in the sky. Then wind moves quickly across the water, spinning over a large space. The whirling wind can cause big waves. Soon heavy rain develops. It's a hurricane!

A hurricane can move onto the land, putting people who live on the coast in danger. It can last for many days. Hurricanes can cause harmful flooding. Usually, many things have been destroyed by the time a hurricane leaves.

Hurricane winds can blow faster than 156 miles per hour!

Cars can get stuck in a snowstorm and driving can be dangerous.

One terrible type of storm happens in the winter. It has strong winds, too. But instead of rain, the water drops freeze as they leave the clouds. They fall as snow and ice. It's a snow storm!

A snow storm can last for many days. If the weather is cold enough, the ice and snow stay on the ground. Even after the storm is over, they will stay until the ground thaws.

In a big storm, families may spend a night in a school, library, or other emergency shelter.

Many things are destroyed in dangerous storms. Of course, people can be injured, too. If a storm is coming, it is important for people to be prepared. It is foolish to say in a storm's path.

Listening to information on a TV or radio is a good idea. People need to gather food, water, and other supplies to last several days. Then everybody should move quickly to a safe place. There is no telling how fast a storm will move. It's also hard to know how long it will last. Weather can have a mind of its own!

Comprehension Check

Summarize

Read "Follow the Weather" again. Then summarize the story.

Think About It

1. Describe what can happen in a thunderstorm. Fill in the Description Chart to help you.

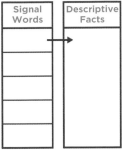

2. How are thunder and lightning related?

3. What can you do to be prepared for a dangerous storm?

4. How is a tornado the same as a hurricane? How are these two storms different?

Write About It

What can people not affected by a storm do to help storm shelters meet the needs of storm victims? Do you think the type of storm would change the needs of the victims? Why?

Skills and Strategies

Decoding

Decode these words. What do you notice about the spellings?

crook	took	owner	shook
goodbye	road	wool	coldest
stood	cookie	football	soot

Vocabulary

introduction   revolves   expose

product   common

Comprehension

AUTHOR'S PURPOSE Authors write to entertain, persuade, or inform.

Use an Author's Purpose chart to list clues about the author's purpose. Then decide why the author wrote the story.

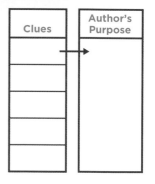

Read "I'm the Best." Identify the author's purpose.

I'm The Best

"Today in art class we will have an introduction to pottery," said Mrs. Tarbrook. "We will use clay and a revolving wheel to make vases."

"I'm the best at using the wheel," Tommy called out.

Mrs. Tarbrook shook her head. "Your classmates might be good at it, too," she replied. "Please begin. I can't wait to look at your finished product."

Tommy went first, but his vase fell apart. Matt made a common bowl that came out perfectly. Tommy said, "I guess other kids can be good at using the wheel, too!"

Make an **Author's Purpose Chart**. Then identify the author's purpose.

Brook's Vase of Good Thoughts

by Armand Reeves

illustrated by Catherine Huerta

Cast
★ Brook   ★ Joan
★ Jimmy   ★ Mr. Woods

Setting
The Greenwood School

Act 1:

MR. WOODS: Because we have a new student, let's have an introduction. Jimmy, please tell us some things about yourself.

JIMMY: Hi. I'm Jimmy. I like football and basketball—lots of action. I don't exactly like art.

BROOK: *(to herself)* Oh, boy.

MR. WOODS: Well, it's nice to meet you, Jimmy. I hope with time you begin to like our class. You may take a seat beside Brook.

JIMMY: Thanks. *(He sits.)*

BROOK: Hi, Jimmy.

(Jimmy does not respond.)

237

MR. WOODS: Class, today we will use dense clay to make vases. We will use a potter's wheel. When the base of the wheel revolves, the vase stays even on top.

JIMMY: Excuse me, Mr. Woods. I don't want to get my wool pants all filthy.

(Other kids laugh.)

JOAN: *(under her breath)* Oh, please.

MR. WOODS: We have smocks. It's best not to wear fancy clothes to art class. You will get them covered in filth! Brook, please help Jimmy pick out a smock.

(Brook and Jimmy go to the cabinet.)

BROOK: Here's a yellow smock.

MR. WOODS: Okay. Let me show you. You have to spin the wheel and keep your fingers wet.

JOAN: Wow. Look at it go!

JIMMY: It still looks messy.

MR. WOODS: Let me tell you a secret. My grandmother told me that I had to think good thoughts. If I didn't, my pottery would not come out right. She explained that clay knew if I didn't care how it turned out.

BROOK: How could clay know?

MR. WOODS: I am not sure. I always try to think about good things while I do this. My pots usually come out fine. *(He shows off a vase.)*

Act 2:

BROOK: What happened to your vase?

JIMMY: I don't know. I still have clay under my fingernails. I worked really hard, and it just fell apart. Maybe my wheel shook too much.

BROOK: Did you think about what Mr. Woods said? He might be right. Maybe the clay knows you don't like it.

JIMMY: Clay is just mud and dirt. It can't feel anything.

(Brook sighs.)

BROOK: Well, I am going to try it anyway.

BROOK: First I'll think of my mother. She is a big help to me. I can talk to her about anything. I am picturing us at the meadow near the woods by my house. It feels good to put my feet in the creek there.

JIMMY: I think it's helping! Your vase looks nice.

BROOK: Good! Next I'll think about my friend Jane. She moved away.

JIMMY: Do you still write to her?

BROOK: Yes! She will be here for my birthday next week.

JIMMY: My birthday is on Monday.

BROOK: So is mine! We have something in common.

BROOK: Now it's finished. I'll put it on the shelf to dry. Then Mr. Woods will bake the vases. That's how they harden. And then we'll paint them.

JIMMY: How does he cook them?

BROOK: I said he has to *bake* them. He uses a kiln. It is a huge oven for pottery.

JIMMY: Look! Another vase fell over! It's destroyed. I guess that kid didn't think good thoughts, either.

(They both laugh.)

Act 3:

BROOK: Jimmy, the vase is ready. Would you like to help paint it?

JIMMY: Well, I do like to paint. And I won't get paint under my fingernails if I can help it!

BROOK: *(laughing)* I like getting dirty. I help my mother in the garden sometimes. Your hands get really dirty if you plant flowers.

MR. WOODS: I see that you two are working together. I can't wait to see your final product!

JIMMY AND BROOK: We can't wait, either!

JIMMY: Do you like this rainbow?

BROOK: Yes! That's absolutely perfect! You're a very good painter.

JIMMY: Do you really believe in all that happiness stuff?

BROOK: I don't know, but we sure made a beautiful vase!

Comprehension Check

Summarize

Read "Brook's Vase of Good Thoughts" again.
Then summarize the story.

Think About It

1. Why do you think the author wrote about what Mr. Woods' grandmother said? Fill in the Author's Purpose Chart to help you.

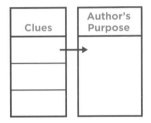

2. What does Brook think of Jimmy at first? What does she think of him at the end?

3. Would you enjoy being friends with a boy like Jimmy? Why or why not?

4. How can a person's attitude help them or hurt them? Explain.

Write About It

Why is it important to become friends with people who are different than you? Explain.

Skills and Strategies

Decoding

Decode these words. What do you notice about the spellings?

rain	land	bank	plane
wood	whale	hook	grass
angry	playful	chatter	flame

Vocabulary

harsh	extreme	inhabited
frequently	contacting	enable

Comprehension

PROBLEM AND SOLUTION In a story, the characters often face a problem. The characters usually solve it by the end of the story. Finding the problem and solution can help you understand which parts of the story are most important.

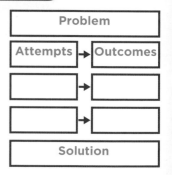

A Problem and Solution Map helps you ask questions to figure out problems and solutions in a selection.

Find the problem that Ernest and his team face.

A Rescue in Antarctica

Years ago, Ernest Shackleton set out to the harshest, coldest place on Earth. He gathered a team and sailed towards Antarctica. Antarctica is extremely cold and uninhabited by humans.

It was a dangerous trip. The ship frequently had to zigzag past huge sheets of ice. One day, the ship got stuck. It wouldn't budge. Ernest saw that he and his crew had to leave the ship.

The men spent over a year searching for help. They had no way to contact anyone. Finally, they reached an island where they found men hunting whales. They were saved! Ernest's leadership enabled them all to survive.

Make a **Problem and Solution Chart**. Use it to help you find a problem and solution for "A Rescue in Antarctica."

The Loneliest Place on Earth

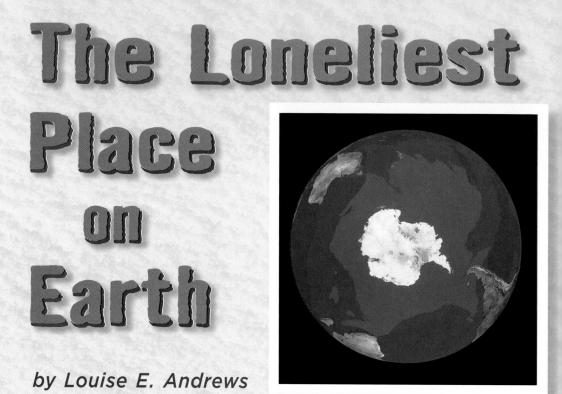

by Louise E. Andrews

A Land of Ice and Snow

The coldest places on Earth are at the extreme ends of the planet. The place at the top of Earth is called the North Pole. It is made up of ice floating on very cold water. The South Pole is at the bottom of the Earth. It is also covered in ice, but under the ice is land. That land is called Antarctica.

If you stand at the South Pole, you can see for miles. But, there isn't much to see besides ice and snow. Antarctica has been called the loneliest place on earth.

Ships can get stuck in ice floes.

Years ago, explorers tried to see if land existed so far south. A trip to the South Pole might sound like fun. Traveling that far south took a long time and was difficult. Rough waves and wind kept the wooden boats from reaching safety. Water froze into chunks of ice, trapping and crushing ships.

Despite the hardships, explorers kept trying to reach the South Pole. No one knows who saw Antarctica first. Almost two hundred years ago, British, Russian, and American sailors all explored close by. Then in 1911, a Norwegian explorer became the first person to reach Antarctica.

Today well-built cruise ships make trips to Antarctica. It can still be a long trip, but it's not as long as it once was. Trips run only during certain months when the weather and conditions are safest.

Glaciers cover most of Antarctica.

You might be surprised to learn that Antarctica is a desert. Antarctica is a desert covered with ice and snow, not sand. However, it gets less precipitation than any place else on earth. Only a few inches of precipitation fall each year.

Antarctica is more than just an unchanging flat field of snow. It has steep ice cliffs. Huge pieces of ice frequently break off, crashing into the sea. Loose sheets of ice move slowly toward the ocean.

In addition, Antarctica has rocky shores, mountain ranges, and even a volcano!

Antarctica's weather is harsh. It's common for temperatures to dip to seventy degrees below zero. Wind can blow at two hundred miles an hour. That's faster than many of the strongest hurricane winds!

Seasons there are unlike most other places. For a few months, the sun shines day and night. At other times during the year, the sun never shines at all.

A snowstorm in Antarctica is very strong. Howling winds pick up loose snow. Clouds of ice crystals form near the ground. Recognizing shapes becomes almost impossible and paths fade away. It is very easy to get lost in an Antarctic snowstorm.

A blizzard covers an expedition camp in 1911.

Can animals and people live in Antarctica? Birds, seals, and whales have a shield against cold air and water. Birds have feathers that trap warm air near their bodies for warmth. Seals have fur and a layer of fat that hold in warmth.

Early explorers had a hard time with the harsh setting. Lives were lost from lack of food and from being exposed to cold weather. Today people know how to prepare to live there. Warmer materials have been made for clothing and shelter. But humans still have a difficult time.

Did you know?...

Interesting facts about how animals survive in Antartica	
Animal	**Feature**
Penguins	have a thick layer of packed waterproof feathers to keep them warm.
Insects	have natural antifeeze in their blood to keep it from freezing.
Seals	are born with white fur to help them blend in to the ice and snow.
Polar Bears	have thick claws to help them dig into the ice so they don't slip.

Penguins are well adapted to the cold in Antarctica.

Visitors can raft in the ice floes at Prospect Point, Antarctica.

Footprints in the Antarctic Snow

Antarctica wasn't inhabited by people for many years. Now a few people stay there for part of the year. At last human footprints lie in the Antarctic snow!

Those who live in Antarctica are scientists. They dress in waterproof coats, snug wool clothes, and boots. They must take what they need with them from home. Supplies can be dropped by planes, but planes may not come very often.

Life in Antarctica can be lonely. The researchers use radios and computers for contacting friends and family.

Why would scientists wish to live near the South Pole? They want to learn more about the coldest place on Earth. Researchers at the South Pole take samples of ice and rocks. They do research that helps them learn about our planet's past. They study animals, birds, and fish that don't exist in any other place on Earth.

Air in Antarctica is thin and clear. The thin air and powerful telescopes enable people to see far into space. Scientists can learn what happens high in the sky.

Scientists also write books and reports describing life near the South Pole. They try to explain why the land must be saved from harm.

Scientists record data to learn about the Earth.

Icebergs float in the sea, but most of the mass is hidden under water.

Many people think that no one should own Antarctica. The land has been saved for the whole world to enjoy.

World leaders have promised to watch over Antarctica. They said they will keep it free from litter and waste. Guests can take photos, but they must leave the land as they found it. People wish to keep Antarctica as it was when explorers first saw it.

Antarctica at sunset.

Antarctica is like no other place in the world. It is a land alive with beauty. It provides a home for interesting animals. It also helps us answer key questions about our planet.

It can be very hard to live in Antarctica. Early explorers felt that all the hardships were worth it. Today's researchers think so, too.

Will you ever visit Antarctica? Who knows? You might even live there one day!

Comprehension Check

Summarize

Reread "The Loneliest Place on Earth." Then summarize the story.

Think About It

1. In the past, why was it hard to get to Antarctica and survive there? Do these problems still exist? Use the Problem and Solution Map to help you.

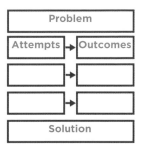

2. Why might drinking water be a problem in Antarctica? How could it be solved?

3. Would you want to visit Antarctica? Why?

4. The land in Antarctica is protected. If it weren't, what changes would we see?

Write About It

Why do you think it is important that no country owns Antarctica by itself? Explain.

Skills and Strategies

Decoding

Decode these words. What do you notice about the vowel spellings?

sick	miss	size	ice
insect	tiger	invent	drive
inch	silent	dinner	inside

Vocabulary

miserable	compressed	grumbled
suggested	eager	

Comprehension

THEME Theme is the overall idea the author wants to tell in a story. Learning the theme will help you understand the story.

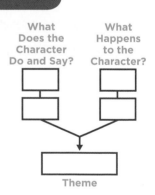

A Theme Chart helps you make inferences and analyze information so you can determine the overall idea the author wants to tell in a story.

Identify the theme.

Miserable Mike

Mike was miserable. He'd carefully compressed his baseball cards into a box and his sister had spilled them. His mom kept asking him to do chores too!

"Why don't you go next door and see if Mrs. Bicker needs anything?" suggested Mike's mom.

"Fine, whatever." Mike grumbled as he stomped next door. Old Mrs. Bicker invited him inside. He spent the next hour looking at her old photographs.

"You've made me so happy," she said eagerly. Mike smiled. Somehow, he felt happier, too.

Make a **Theme Chart** for "Miserable Mike." Use it to find the theme of the story.

The Perfect Ingredient

by Margaret Mertz

illustrated by Christy Hale

Less of This and Less of That

"Kim! Nila! It's dinnertime!" Mom called. "You know what to do!"

It was Dad's turn to cook. It was always our turn to set the table.

I put out salad. Nila rolled her eyes. "Salad *again*," she complained.

Spring rain tapped at the windows. I shrugged. There would be salad every night this week. We might have a little meat, sauce, or some noodles. But there was no butter, cheese, or ice cream like we used to have so frequently.

"I don't like being hungry," Nila whined. "I'm not fat."

"None of us are," I said. "And we're not really hungry. There's plenty of food."

I knew what she meant. Dad had been sick. The doctor said he had to cut out salt and fat. Then Mom said that it would be good for all of us. "You don't want to get sick too, Kim," she said.

She was right. It would make Dad miserable if we ate sweets and he couldn't. I'm sure Dad missed the snacks he had eaten before.

Dinner tasted okay. But I still missed mashed potatoes and gravy. I didn't want to make things harder for Dad. But I sure wanted something sweet.

Then I had an idea. I could make a treat that would be good for us. Something like oatmeal cookies with chewy sweet raisins would be good. I could almost taste them now.

I was eager to get started on my tasty dessert. I told Mom about my plan.

"Try the back cabinet. That's where I keep the spices. Let me know if you need help..." she winked.

Right away the plan went wrong. I had forgotten about that little pest Nila. She saw me looking at a cookbook.

"Cookies? Pie? I want some too!" she said. "Give me some, or I'll tell."

I sensed a scream coming. "I am going to try to make some cookies," I said.

"Can I help?" asked Nila.

She would plead until she got her way. "Okay," I grumbled. "You can be my helper."

"No! I want to be your baking *partner*."

What could I do? I needed her cooperation.

Nila and I brainstormed. We talked about the things we loved to eat.

"Brownies!" exclaimed Nila. "Let's try peppermint ice cream. Can we make that?"

"Those have too much sugar and fat. So does everything in this book. We have to invent a new food. We could try something with fruit. We all like fruit." I looked for aprons, pans, and other equipment.

"What are we going to make?" Nila asked.

"I don't know yet," I said. "It will be a mystery treat."

A Strange Recipe

In the back of the spice cabinet I found a dusty old jar. The label read *The Perfect Ingredient.* Inside were sparkly crystals, like salt.

I dipped my finger inside and put some in my mouth. "Mmmm! Oatmeal raisin cookies! Nila, have some!"

Nila dipped her finger into the jar. When she put it in her mouth, her eyes opened wide. "Peppermint ice cream!" she said. The crystals tasted exactly like the foods we were craving!

"This will be perfect!" I cried. "There's a tube of rolls in the fridge, and milk and eggs. If we add this and bake it, then everyone will have the dessert they've been craving!"

"Okay, partner," I said, "You sift some flour and sprinkle it on the baking pan. Let's start cooking."

I gave Nila flour and eggs. "Here," I said. "Add two eggs. I'll get the pan ready."

Soon the kitchen was a mess. Flour and eggshells were everywhere. And the milk pitcher left a sticky ring in the white powder.

"How much should I make?" asked Nila.

"Just make sure it's a lot so we all get some."

I cut and compressed the rolls in the pan.

"Mix the flour with the egg and milk," I said. "Don't use too much liquid." It looked runny.

I found low fat cream cheese in the refrigerator. "Mix this with the crystals," I said. "The cream cheese should make the product sweeter."

"I can also add extra flour to make it thicker," Nila suggested.

I spread the cream cheese mixture on each roll. "I know!" Nila said excitedly. "Now we roll them up and bake them!"

"And we watch so they don't burn," I added.

The roll-ups baked to a golden brown. I poured more crystals on top. "There!" I said. "Let's show Mom and Dad."

Mom and Dad were at the table, looking at the kitchen door. When I walked out, Mom asked, "How did it go?"

"Great! We made rolls for all of us," I said quickly. "Don't worry. We made them with low fat foods and no sugar. We can all eat it!" I smiled and held my breath. That was mostly the truth!

"Extremely delicious! What are they called?" Dad asked.

I thought quickly. "Mystery Treats!"

"That is the *perfect* name," said mom, knowingly.

Comprehension Check

Summarize

Read "The Perfect Ingredient" again. Then summarize the story.

Think About It

1. What message do you think the author is trying to get across by having the sisters work together? Fill in the Theme Chart to help you find the theme.

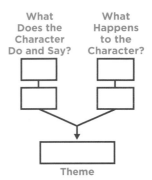

2. In the beginning, did Kim want to work with her sister on the dessert? How do you know?

3. Why is it important to eat healthy foods?

4. Was it a good decision to use an ingredient that the girls didn't know? Explain.

Write About It

What else can people do to keep healthy and fit besides eating healthy foods? Explain.

Skills and Strategies

Decoding

Decode these words. What do you notice about the spellings?

sweet	test	shred	bleed
fever	desert	bench	treat
sneak	after	scream	elbow

Vocabulary

available	reduce	scents
preparation	precise	

Comprehension

CAUSE AND EFFECT A cause is something that makes an action happen. An effect is the action that follows the cause.

Cause → Effect
→
→
→
→

A Cause and Effect Chart helps you ask questions to figure out what happens in a story (an effect) and why it happens (a cause).

Identify the causes and effects.

Funny Ways to Feel Better

Long ago, people didn't have medicines like we have today. They used what was available, such as wild plants, to cure illnesses. Some things that they did might sound funny to us.

To reduce the pain of a sore throat, people tied eel skins around their necks. People who had trouble sleeping would burn scented candles by their beds.

Today we prepare real medicines to heal our sicknesses. Scientists use precise amounts of plants in some medicines. However, the silly cures are still amusing to hear about!

Make a **Cause and Effect Chart** for "Funny Ways to Feel Better." Use it to help you find the causes and effects in the passage.

Plants THAT CAN Heal

BY AMBER BERNSTEIN

Where Do We Get Medicine?

Picture a garden filled with spring flowers. People enjoy the bright colors and sweet scents. Just looking at flowers can make people feel better.

That's not the only way flowers and other plants make people feel better. Throughout history, people have used plants to cure ailments. Long ago, many people believed that some plants had special powers. Modern scientists know that this is not just a guess. Some plants really do have the power to heal diseases. Medicines made from plants can help relieve pain and cure illness.

Scientists gather plants from nature and test them. They are eager to discover which parts can be used in medicines. Then those parts are studied in laboratories to make sure they're safe. The elements can then be made into medicine.

Measurements must be very precise. If the combination is too weak, it won't work. If it is too strong, it can make someone more sick than before. The exact preparation needs to be known.

A scientist examines each plant carefully.

Incredible Plants

Plant medicines can cure diseases that have been around for a long time. For many years, people tried to find a cure for *swamp fever*. It struck people who inhabited or worked in the jungle. People thought that swamp fever was caused by dirty air. It was really caused by insect bites.

Those who were sick were miserable. They had fever, horrible chills, and muscle pains. Many of the sick were hospitalized, and a large number of them died. No one knew a cure for the sickness.

When an insect bites, it swallows some of the blood from its victim. If the blood has a disease in it, like swamp fever, the insects next victim will get that disease.

Solving the problem wasn't easy. People tried to drain the swamps. Killing the insects didn't work because there were too many of them. A medicine that could prevent, treat, or cure swamp fever was needed.

This medicine was found in nature. For years people in South America used a white powder to lower fevers. The powder was made from the wood of a particular rain forest tree. Doctors found that the powder worked on swamp fever, too! It protected healthy people from getting sick. It also cured those who were already sick. With this discovery people could safely travel and work in the jungle.

Rainforests like these are filled with rare and interesting plants. Some of them can be used to make medicines.

Some plants are used to make medicines that people take every day. Aspirin is a common medicine that is used to reduce pain and fevers. It is made from the leaves of a willow tree. Before aspirin was available, tea from willow leaves was used to reduce pain. Now the leaves are made into little white pills in a laboratory.

Another common plant medicine is aloe. Aloe is used to treat simple burns such as sunburn. Many people keep an aloe plant at home just like any other houseplant. But if someone gets a burn from a stove, the aloe can help. Just pop open the plant's smooth leaves, and rub the gel on the burn.

This is the leaf of an aloe plant that has been broken. The gel on the inside can help heal light burns.

When Things Are Not As They Seem

Not all plants are good for you. Plants such as poison ivy can give people bad rashes.

Watch out! This is a poison ivy plant. Many campers and hikers make sure to stay far away from this plant.

For a long time, people thought that tomatoes were poisonous. The tomato is related to toxic plants such as deadly nightshade. So people were fooled into thinking that tomatoes were dangerous, too.

Years ago, a man decided to prove that tomatoes are safe to eat. He stood in public and announced that he would eat a tomato. A crowd of people came to watch. They were shocked when he ate it and still lived!

Today, tomatoes are made into many foods that we eat everyday. These include spaghetti sauce and ketchup. Not only are tomatoes not poisonous, they're actually good for you!

It's hard to believe that people once thought a simple food like this was poisonous.

While we now know that smoking tobacco is bad for you, it may be possible to use tobacco in helpful ways.

Long ago people thought that tobacco was good for you, too. Tobacco plants were used by Native Americans to reduce pain and cure colds. Later, people around the world tried smoking tobacco leaves to cure sicknesses. They thought that tobacco could fix everything from tooth pain to cancer.

We now know that smoking tobacco does not cure cancer. It can actually cause it. It can give people heart and brain problems, too. Just being in a room with tobacco smoke can be harmful.

Scientists are trying to find new ways to use tobacco safely. In the future, tobacco plants may be used in perfumes or insect sprays.

Plants used in medicines can be found all over the world. Many come from rain forest plants, while others grow on farms. The plant shown here is used to help treat cancer in children. This plant once grew in the wild. Now whole crops of it are grown in large fields.

Would you ever guess that this bright flower holds a powerful medicine within it?

Every year we find more medicines hidden inside of plants. Scientists are looking from the ocean to the desert for new cures. Each time they find another cure, they're helping people live happier, healthier lives.

Comprehension Check

Summarize

Reread "Plants That Can Heal." Then summarize the selection.

Think About It

1. How can plants help people? Fill in the Cause and Effect Chart to help you.

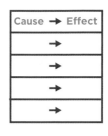

2. Why do you think people turned to nature to find medicine? Explain.

3. Would you enjoy being a scientist who searches for plants to cure people? Why?

4. Reread "Large Trees with Large Jobs" on pages 81–84. Why is it important for us to grow our own medicines instead of just collecting them from rainforests? Explain.

Write About It

In the United States, we can make medicines to cure diseases. Should we share these medicines with countries that do not have enough money to make them? Why?

Skills and Strategies

Decoding

Decode these words. What do you notice about the spellings?

lost	groan	pony	clock
towboat	bottle	follow	phone
oak	cost	over	drop

Vocabulary

inappropriate   treasure   impatiently

situations   irregular

Comprehension

AUTHOR'S PERSPECTIVE Each author has their own way of looking at a subject. This point of view is called the author's perspective.

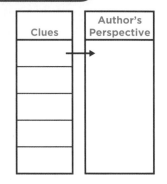

An Author's Perspective Chart helps you ask questions to find clues to the author's opinion or point of view. Use your chart to figure out the author's perspective.

Identify the author's perspective.

Pirate Molly Does a Good Job

The prisoners began to struggle. This was inappropriate. They should have sat still and let the pirates take their treasure to avoid being hurt. Pirate Molly and her crew were growing impatient. "Show us the treasure!" Molly roared. The situation felt tense.

Finally, the prisoners showed the pirates where to dig. When Pirate Molly pulled out the chest, her crew hollered. The chest was filled with special gold coins with irregular patterns.

Pirate Molly finally got what she was owed. She'd been paid in gold for a job she had done well.

Make an **Author's Perspective Chart**. Then identify the author's perspective.

Joe and Nicole
Crack the Code

by Betsy Donaldson

illustrated by
Cathy Morrison

Inside an Old Bottle

"Okay, class, listen up," said Ms. Jones. "I have a project for you to work on over the weekend."

"Homework?" asked Joe. "On the weekend?"

His twin sister, Nicole, watched him sadly. She wished he wouldn't call out in class. It was inappropriate. The two of them were twins, but they were very different.

"I want you to find something from your family's history," said Ms. Jones. "It might be a clock your grandfather owned or an old letter. Then describe in writing what it means to you. This is due on Monday."

That night, Joe and Nicole climbed up the irregular attic stairs. Boxes sat in messy piles all over. The twins looked at each other. Who knew what could be hidden in there?

"What a spooky room," said Joe. "I bet an invisible monster lives here!"

"It's just a gloomy old attic," replied Nicole. "Bring that flashlight and help me over here."

"Look!" said Joe. "Here are some old toys."

"Wow!" exclaimed Nicole. "There's our old train set." As she reached for it, her foot pushed up a floorboard.

"What's that?" asked Joe. The twins saw something dusty in the hole beneath the floor.

"It's just an old bottle," sighed Nicole. "Let's keep looking for an object for our report."

"This is incredible!" Joe exclaimed. "Maybe it's filled with something exciting!"

"Maybe somebody just missed the trash can," said Nicole. "It's only a bottle."

Joe still liked his idea better. "Look!" he said again. "There are papers inside it. Whoever left it here was sending a secret message. Maybe a cowboy wrote down the location of a lost mine. Maybe one of the papers is a map to a royal treasure."

"Oh, Joe," said Nicole. She sighed. "They're probably just old letters or something. You always dream up these impossible situations. Open your notebook and let's get busy." She squinted at the bottle. "The glass looks cloudy. It must be old."

The twins opened the bottle and tugged on the papers. The faded yellow papers crinkled in their hands. They had to be careful not to tear them.

"I don't understand this!" Nicole whispered. "I know these words aren't in the dictionary."

"I told you it was a secret message!" shouted Joe. "It's in code and we have to crack it. Then you'll see proof that I'm right. It's going to be directions to hidden pirate gold!"

"If you say so," replied Nicole. "Let's go ask Mom and Dad if they recognize the handwriting."

Uncle Bobby's Treasure

The twins asked their mom if she knew who wrote the letters. She slowly unrolled each paper. They watched her impatiently.

"I do know who wrote these!" Mom said. "That's Bobby's handwriting."

"When I was little, my brother Bobby and I loved writing codes. When my grandfather was in the army he sent coded messages. Once he sent a warning to prepare his unit for a surprise attack. He saved their lives. He showed Uncle Bobby and me how to make our own codes."

"So what does this letter say?" asked Nicole eagerly.

"I have no idea," said Mom. "Call Uncle Bobby. He might remember."

Joe and Nicole ran to the phone.

"Sorry," said Uncle Bobby. "I'm really busy right now with my new job. I wish I could help, but I don't have time. Most codes I wrote as a kid were simple, though."

"Try looking for patterns in the words," suggested Uncle Bobby. "The letters E, T, and S are used the most in English. Replace the most common letters with those. You might be able to guess a few words. Then maybe you'll be able to understand the whole thing."

Joe and Nicole worked hard. At last, they cracked the code.

"Treasure!" the letter began, "Buried treasure on east side of old oak tree in Rockglen Park. See X on tree's trunk."

Joe gasped. "I know that tree! It's by the field near the swings!"

Joe and Nicole raced to the park, kneeled by the tree, and began digging. Finally, they felt something hard. They had found a box!

Joe slowly lifted the lid. Inside was a thick book. "Army Codes" was written on its front. Nicole flipped through pages and pages of codes.

"Treasure?" said Joe. "It's just an old book."

"Maybe Mom knows what it is," said Nicole.

Mom smiled when she saw the box. "This thing brings back memories," she said. "It belonged to my grandfather. He died when I was very little. He must have given it to Bobby."

Mom got up and hugged each of them. Nicole saw that her eyes were wet with tears.

"Well," sighed Joe. "At least we have something to write about for our homework. I still wish we'd found a treasure, though."

"Do you know what?" asked Nicole, smiling. "I think we did. We found a family treasure!"

Comprehension Check

Summarize

Read "Joe and Nicole Crack the Code" again. Then summarize the story.

Think About It

1. Fill in the Author's Perspective Chart to explain why information about the great-grandfather is important.

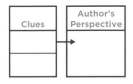

2. Use details from the story to explain how Joe and Nicole are different and alike.
3. What treasures are important to your family? Explain your answer.
4. Why does Nicole think that the box really is a treasure?

Write About It

Why might people want to write in code? Explain a situation where writing in code could be useful.

Skills and Strategies

Decoding

Decode these words. What do you notice about the spellings?

wood	loose	cook	proof
shampoo	goodnight	notebook	boost
dogwood	soon	stood	lookout

Vocabulary

reflection	vanished	majesty
depend	delicious	

Comprehension

SUMMARIZE Summarizing a story means retelling it in your own words. A summary should include

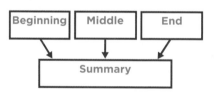

only the most important points in the story. Summarizing helps you understand the story.

A Summary Chart helps you answer questions about what happens at the beginning, middle, and end of the story. Make a Summary Chart and use it to summarize the selection.

Summarize the passage.

The Lesson

Moona knelt down by the sea and looked into the cool water. Her reflection stared back. "I miss my big sister," she told her reflection. "I wish Pooja was here to read school books to me." She took a stone and threw it into the water. Her reflection vanished with the rippling water.

Just then, she saw a pod of whales swim by. With grace and majesty, they jumped in the water. She heard tiny whistles as they talked.

Suddenly, she stood up. "I get the message! Those whales are reminding me that I can still depend on my family. I can speak to them in my thoughts even if they aren't all really here!" she said. "Seeing those whales helped me!"

Make a **Summary Chart**. Then use it to help you put the passage in your own words.

Proof of Goodness

by Laurel Keats
illustrated by Dennis Albetski

Soon You Will Understand

There was a time when the northern lands were still clean. No cars made tracks through the snow. No planes left trails in the clear blue sky. Life was not easy, but the people had what they needed.

In that time, a family lived in a small wooden cabin on the bay. Rose lived with her grandchildren, Byron and Holly, whom she raised.

Rose taught Byron and Holly all they needed to know. She taught them to melt snow for cooking and laundry. She taught them to use waterproof skin from seals to make warm clothes. She helped them carve pointed spears so they could hunt for meat.

One day as the three of them worked together, Rose told Byron and Holly something important. It was about the whales that lived far out in the sea. "We depend on the whales," she told them. "They are a treasure. They give us meat to eat all winter. They give us their bones so we can make tiny needles and big boats. They give us oil so that we will have light available all winter."

All of the townspeople depended on the whales, too. When a hunting trip went well, they had a big feast. Each family brought food that they had traded for or caught. They boiled fish and prepared bear meat with delicious sauces.

Then the people sang, danced and told stories. They talked about the whales and hunting. They clapped for the best songs and stories. Under the glowing moon, everyone joined the dancing around the campfire.

But that year Rose did not enjoy the feast. She sat by herself and looked like she was in a sad mood.

After the feast, Rose returned to the cabin
with Byron and Holly. She paused and stood by
the window. She looked out at the white snow and
thought. She said, "I am very old. Soon I will go up
to rest with the Great Woman in the sky."

"No," Byron said impatiently. "You will live many
more years."

"That is incorrect," the old woman said. "Before
long I will die. That is how it must be. Do not worry,
little one. I will never be apart from you." She
looked down at him. "Soon you will understand."

Byron had a hard time falling asleep that night. In the darkness of his dreams, he walked down to the bay through the mist and fog. Byron thought he could see an irregular shape beneath the water. He felt a strange attraction to it. *I cannot go without confirming what the shape is*, he thought.

At first Byron thought he saw his grandmother swimming in the icy water. As he watched, her shape turned into that of a whale. It was a narwhal, a whale that has a long twisted tooth. Suddenly, the shape that was both his grandmother and the whale vanished.

When Byron woke up the next morning, Rose had died.

Byron and Holly were very sad. Another family took them in and was very kind to them. But it was not the same as when Grandmother Rose was alive. Byron fought his feelings of sadness as hard as he could.

One day Byron decided to go hunting along the bay. *I will look at the sea and think about her,* he thought. *Maybe then I will understand what she meant about always being with me.*

Byron walked towards the bay, squinting at the sun's reflection on the snow.

   As Byron got near the bay, he gazed into the distance. Something was out there. The shape moved closer and closer. It grew bigger and bigger. Byron slowly approached the water's edge.

   At last the creature broke the water's surface. Byron found himself looking at a giant narwhal. It was the biggest one he had ever seen!

With a splashing sound, a second narwhal joined the first. They swam alongside each other, gliding down the bay. They had the majesty of whales, but the grace of soaring birds.

Byron stared at the two narwhals. He knew that such large creatures could feed the townspeople for weeks. He should run back and get the hunters.

But he couldn't. Byron remembered his dream about Grandmother Rose and the narwhal. He watched them swim until they disappeared out to sea.

Byron rushed back to town and found his sister. "I know what Grandmother Rose was trying to tell us!" he shouted. "I see her swimming when I see the whales."

"What do you mean?" asked Holly.

"She said that she will always be with us," said Byron. "I didn't understand it then. How could she be with us if she wasn't alive? How foolish of me! Now I understand."

He went on, "She is with us in the spears that we carve. She is with us in the snow that gives us water. She is with us in the beauty of the narwhals. She put a bit of herself into all that she taught us. She will always be with us!"

Comprehension Check

Summarize

Read "Proof of Goodness"
again. Then summarize
the story.

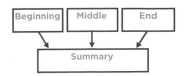

Think About It

1. What did Byron eventually learn about
   his grandmother?
2. How did Byron feel about his grandmother?
   Explain how you know.
3. Explain an important lesson that you learned
   from a family member.
4. Reread "Joe and Nicole Crack the Code" on
   pages 291–292. How do Joe and Nicole, like
   Byron, learn a lesson about their family? Use
   details from each story to explain your answer.

Write About It

Think of someone in history who "lives on."
Explain how they were important and how their
work or memory is still important to us today.

Skills and Strategies

Decoding

Decode these words. What do you notice about the spellings?

turn	table	motor	bird
blister	garden	possible	sadden
doctor	important	travel	hesitant

Vocabulary

| peculiar | communicate | innocent |
| bustling | deserve | |

Comprehension

SEQUENCE The sequence of events is the order in which things happen. Knowing the order of the events helps you understand the story.

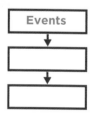

As you read, take note of the order of events in the story. Use a Sequence Chart to show the sequence of events.

Identify the order of events.

Caught in the Act

Jim was walking through a bustling farmers' market, shopping for the week. Near a pumpkin stand, he saw a peculiar sight. Two birds looked like they were trying to communicate. He came closer

Jim couldn't believe what he heard. "We deserve some fun," one bird said.

"You fly around in front and look innocent. I'll grab a lady's purse," said the other.

"No you won't!" yelled Jim. Both birds squawked and flew away!

Make a **Sequence Chart** for "The Bird Thief." Then use it to help you summarize the story.

The Girl Who Talked to Animals

by Julia Garcia

illustrated by John Hovell

Arden's Rare Talent

Arden had a very rare talent. She could talk to animals, and she could hear them, too.

All over town, Arden saw animals doing peculiar things that confused most people. When sheep got thirsty they would hop on their hind legs. The farmers didn't know what was wrong with them. Insects were eating all of the food in the fields. Then, the people had nothing left to eat. Friendly dogs would bark until people ran away.

One day Arden took a long trip to see the king and queen. She wanted to tell them how her talent could help the town.

THIS WAY TO THE ROYAL PALACE →

Arden got to the palace that afternoon.
The king and queen wore fancy clothes and gold
crowns. Arden explained her plan to them. She
was confident that they would like it.

"I can speak with the animals and tell them to
behave," said Arden. "I can keep them from tearing
up gardens and farms. I can tell unpleasant animals
to stay far from people. I can even explain why the
animals are acting this way."

"She's lying!" said the king. "No one can speak
with a wild beast."

"That's impossible!" agreed the queen
impatiently. "Send this foolish girl away."

Arden left the palace. She walked down the noisy city streets bustling with birds and animals. Arden stopped to hear what they were saying.

A horse stopped and tugged at its reins.

"Ouch!" Arden heard it say. "I have a pebble stuck in my shoe."

The soldier riding the horse did not know why he had stopped. He tapped the horse with his foot, but it stood still. "Why are you just standing here?" asked the soldier, tapping it again.

Then a bird flew from the top of a window and cawed loudly. Arden understood that it said, "Stay away from my nest!" The sound scared a baby, making it cry. The bird flew towards the baby's grandfather and tried grabbing his beard. "What is wrong with this bird?" he shouted.

"I can help," Arden told the crowd hesitantly. "The horse needs a doctor for its hoof. The bird is making a home near those windows. It just doesn't want people near its nest."

The soldier frowned. "There's a law against telling lies, little girl," he said. "You had better keep quiet."

The soldier dragged Arden to a dark and cold jail cell. Arden sat down and sobbed.

"I just wanted to help," she cried. "Why doesn't anyone trust me?

A soldier pushed two black dogs into Arden's jail cell. "Here, tell your troubles to these dogs. Maybe they'll believe you, since no one else will," he said.

"That's right," chuckled the jailer, who had just arrived. "See if they understand you and then maybe they'll set you free."

Arden cried all night until the sun rose. Then, she dried her eyes. She had an idea.

Arden Becomes a Legend

There was a garden in the kingdom, filled with flowers and birds. The birds had fruit to eat and branches to rest on. The birds also had plenty of room to fly. A gardener took care of the bird garden. She made sure that the birds were safe and happy.

That night, the birds woke up to the sound of howling. The black dogs were explaining how Arden ended up in jail. The birds felt badly when they heard what had happened to Arden.

"She just wanted to help the animals," they squawked. "Now it's our turn to help her." The birds rose up to the sky and flew off.

The next day, the gardener asked to see the king and queen. She was upset. "The little girl told the truth," she said. "She really can communicate with animals. I'm sorry to tell you this, but the birds rose up to the sky and vanished this morning. They found the jailer's keys and took them to free the girl."

"So she told the truth?" asked the king.

"I think she did your majesty," replied the gardener. "If not, how would my birds have known to set her free?"

"If she was truthful, then she didn't break the law," said the king. "That means that she doesn't deserve to be in jail at all."

When the birds freed her, Arden considered leaving the kingdom. But, to her surprise, the king and queen declared that she was innocent.

"We now know that you really can speak with animals," they said. "We would love it if you'd help us understand our animals. We're sorry we didn't depend on you or trust you. Please, let us give you a reward. Ask for any treasure, and it will be yours."

At first, Arden didn't want to ask for anything. Then, she asked, "Can I keep the two dogs that saved me?"

"Of course," they replied.

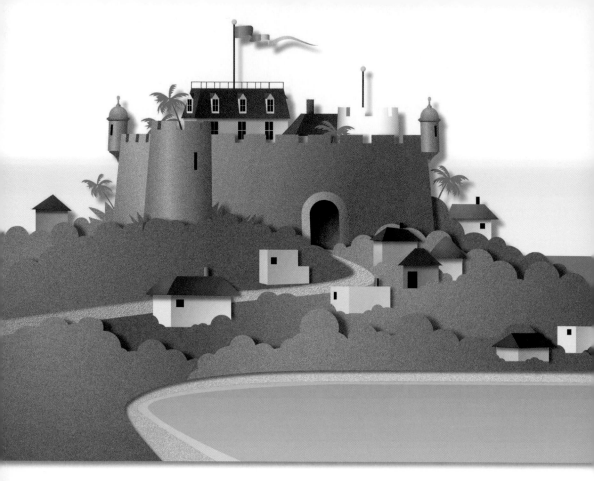

Arden went to work for the king and queen. She helped people and animals understand each other. Soon the kingdom became a nicer place to live.

"We're glad there's someone who can speak with the animals," the people said. "It's so important. Now we can all lead peaceful lives together." The king and queen were happy, too.

The little girl who talked to animals became a legend. Most *people* who hear this story think that it's made up. It's only the *animals* that know the truth!

Comprehension Check

Summarize

Reread "The Girl Who Talked to Animals." Fill in The Sequence Chart. Then summarize the story.

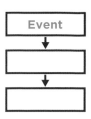

Event
↓
↓

Think About It

1. How did Arden get out of jail? Tell each step she took to get help.
2. What kind of person is the king? How does he change in the story?
3. If you could talk with something besides people, what would you want it to be? Explain your answer.
4. Why is it important to find out if someone is telling the truth before you make a judgment?

Write About It

Do you think it's good to stand up for what's right, like the gardener did in the story, even if it might not be popular? Explain your answer.

Skills and Strategies

Decoding

Decode these words. What do you notice about the spellings?

growl	owl	ground	loud
proud	outdoor	ounce	powder
bound	shower	towel	downhill

Vocabulary

eerie	surrounded	scuttle
secure	concluded	

Comprehension

MAKE JUDGMENTS You learn about characters by thinking about what they say and do. This can help you make judgments about the characters and the story.

Action → Judgment	
→	
→	
→	
→	

A Judgments Chart helps you judge whether or not a character's actions are a good idea.

Make judgments about Todd and Amber.

A Lot to Learn

"It's eerie in here," said Todd. He was down in a cave with some pals. Long, thin stones surrounded them. They seemed to drip from the roof of the cave to the ground.

"Oh, you're scared?" teased Amber. "Why? It's so interesting in here!" Suddenly, a little animal scuttled over the cave floor. Amber jumped and grabbed for a round stone. She held on securely.

"Wow, are you okay?" asked Todd. "No broken bones," Amber concluded, smiling as she blushed. She thought, "I guess I shouldn't be so quick to joke about others!"

Create a **Judgments Chart**. Then make judgments about what happened in the story.

An Outdoor Adventure

by Max Foster
illustrated by Nancy J. Starosky

Nothing to Be Proud of

"This will be the best trip ever!" Becky said as she sat down.

Her older brother Lance and her Uncle Logan were at the table. They had to agree. Lance didn't even mind that his kid sister would be with them. The three of them would be camping alone in a national park. Becky and Lance's parents would be nearby at a meeting.

"Now, don't worry," Mom said. "We'll be staying at the hotel down the road if you need us."

"It'll be nice for you to spend time together," added Dad. "Camping can teach you about looking out for each other."

After breakfast, they all drove to Big Bend. They found the perfect spot to pitch their tent. It was in a clearing surrounded by tall trees.

"Can you give me a hand over here?" asked Mom. Becky helped her unroll the huge tent. Uncle Logan held the tent pins secure while Dad hammered them. Soon the tent was fastened to the ground.

"Fantastic job!" said Dad, smiling. "Well, I guess it's time for us to go to the hotel. We must make it back in time for the meeting."

Becky smiled, but she wished they could stay.

"Let's roast marshmallows," suggested Lance after their parents had left.

"We'll need to find some sticks," said Uncle Logan. He picked up a few and split them in half. "Of course, marshmallows may attract bears."

Becky gasped. "But Mom said there aren't any scary animals here," she said.

"There may be a skunk!" Lance said. "Remember when Walter's dog ran into one?

"He got sprayed badly," Uncle Logan said.

"You should've seen him scuttle back to camp!" laughed Lance. "Really, you didn't need to see him. You could smell him!" Lance laughed loudly.

"Lots of funny things can happen on camping trips," said Uncle Logan. "Remember when we told your friend Josh that the campsite was haunted?"

"Yeah," Lance added. "We told him a scary story about animals that lived in the trees." Lance held his flashlight under his chin so his face looked eerie.

"He jumped every time he heard an owl," Uncle Logan said with childlike delight. "He almost didn't sleep at all because we kept scaring him!"

"That's nothing to be proud of," said Becky, folding her arms. "You guys aren't funny. You're just mean."

Becky grabbed a raincoat from her bag and stomped off. "I want to be alone she said.

"It's only innocent fun," protested Uncle Logan. Becky kept walking. Uncle Logan shrugged. "Don't go far," he said.

Becky vanished and didn't answer him. Soon a gentle rain tapped on the leaves. The trail was soft from the rain that had fallen that summer.

The raindrops became louder as they fell harder to the ground. Becky grew distracted and left the muddy trail.

Suddenly the ground gave way beneath Becky. A rush of water swept her downhill. "I'm going to drown!" she yelled.

Lance and Uncle Logan to the Rescue

Lance and Uncle Logan heard something over the sound of the rain. "Was that Becky?" Lance asked.

Uncle Logan's face was white, and his eyes were wide.

Lance and Uncle Logan raced down the trail. They came to the spot where the ground had washed away.

"Becky!" shouted Lance. No one answered.

"There she is! Down on that ledge!" yelled Uncle Logan. It was hard for them to communicate over the howling wind.

Lance lowered Uncle Logan down to the ledge. "It's our fault," Uncle Logan concluded. "Your parents depended on us, and we let her go on her own."

When Uncle Logan reached her, Becky started crying. "Stay calm," he said confidently as he held Becky's hand. "We'll get you out of here somehow."

"This slope is too slippery to climb," Lance said. We'll have to walk farther downhill. Then tomorrow we can find our way back."

"We'll need to find a place to sleep tonight," Uncle Logan said.

"Why don't we look for a resting place, before it gets too dark? Then we can dry off," said Lance.

"You go first, Lance," said Becky. "Make sure to check for wild beasts and skunks."

Lance spotted a flat rock covered with dead leaves and branches. It was just like a cave. "Let's crawl under here," he said. "At least we'll be dry."

When the rain stopped, the sound of tree frogs was the only noise outside.

"Try to get some sleep, Becky," said Uncle Logan. "Don't worry. We'll get back to our campsite tomorrow."

The kids woke up early the next day. The ground was still soft, but it had dried a bit. They climbed back up the slope and then toward their tent.

"We should hurry!" warned Uncle Logan. "We've got to make it back to camp before your parents do."

Just as they found the tent, Becky heard her parents' voices. She ran towards them and gave Mom a big hug.

"Mom! Dad!" she cried. "Guess what happened?"

Lance and Uncle Logan looked at each other with fear in their eyes. Would she retell the story placing the blame on them? If so, Lance would say that they were innocent!

"I almost got lost," said Becky. "Then Lance and Uncle Logan came and saved me. I am lucky that I have a brother and an uncle like them!"

Comprehension Check

Summarize

Read "An Outdoor Adventure" again. Then summarize the story.

Think About It

1. At first, what do Lance and Uncle Logan's words and actions show about them? Use the Judgments Chart to help you answer.

Action → Judgment
→
→
→
→

2. How did Lance and Uncle Logan feel when Becky saw her parents at the end of the story? How do you know?

3. Which character are you most like? Why?

4. Why do you think Becky didn't tell her parents about how she wandered off? Explain.

Write About It

Becky's father said camping can teach you to look out for each other. What do you think he meant? Explain.

Skills and Strategies

Decoding

Decode these words. What do you notice about the spellings?

photo	short	truth	bathtub
thrill	whisper	whine	nephew
whirl	punish	pamphlet	marshmallow

Vocabulary

anxious	gestures	witness
thrive	halt	

Comprehension

PERSUASION Persuasion is a way to convince others to act or think in a certain way.

Word or Phrase	Technique

To help you decide whether you agree with the author's ideas, use a Persuasion Chart.

Identify the persuasive techniques. Do you think that the author's point in this paragraph is believable?

Stopping a Bully

Sometimes when people are anxious or upset, they can act in a mean way. People may make rude gestures toward somebody else. They might yell nasty names at their pals. Some people may even hit or punch other kids. Even if a person is usually nice, anyone who does these things is acting like a bully.

If you witness something like this, or if it happens to you, don't shout back. It might be better to just walk away. Bullies thrive on attention. If you stop paying attention to them, it will help to halt the bullying.

Make a **Persuasion Chart** for "Stopping a Bully." Decide whether the author was able to convince you about their point.

The Truth About Bullies

by Sue Reilly

What Are the Facts?

Everyone in school knows about bullies. But not everything people say about bullies is true. Before we can rid our schools of bullying, we need the facts. Here is some of what we know about bullies and bullying.

Bullying is a big deal. Thousands of kids in this country are bullied every day. Someone is bullied on a playground once every seven minutes. In classrooms, bullying happens about twice every hour. Bullying makes kids fearful, anxious, and even leads to absence from school. No one learns well in a school where they are surrounded by bullying.

Words can hurt. "Sticks and stones may break my bones, but names will never hurt me." This is a common phrase that isn't always true. Words do not cause physical injury, but they can be hurtful.

You know that hitting someone does harm to them. So if you got mad, you know not to hit another person.

Using words to hurt is wrong too. Bullies might say mean things or make teasing faces and gestures. Bullies may tease kids for being too short, too smart, or too slow. These words can be upsetting for a very long time.

Kids that are bullied may pretend to be sick to stay home from school. But that just makes them more upset.

Bullying can happen anywhere – in the classroom, the hallways, or even the playground.

You cannot always just ignore a bully. Some people say that if you ignore bullies, they will go away. This doesn't always work because bullies thrive on attention. If they don't get it, they are likely to keep bullying. Then the bullying might get more vicious.

Some bullies do not believe that they are hurting others. They might say they were joking or that their teasing is funny. They might not see the damage they are doing. But it is never a joke to hurt someone else.

334

Girls can be bullies, too. Anyone can be a bully. Girls may not hit, push, or threaten other kids as much as boys do. However, girls often bother others with mean words.

Girls sometimes even attack with silence. They might ignore certain kids or not let them into games. Kids who are treated this way feel separate and alone.

Bullying does not just happen in school. It also happens on the way to and from school. Kids are teased and bullied at parks and club meetings. Some bullies even use computers to attack by posting mean things.

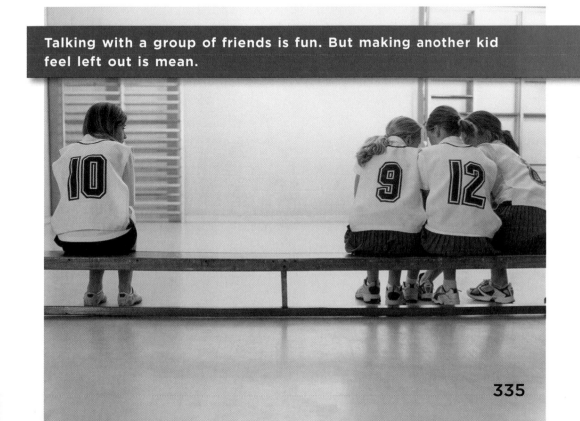

Talking with a group of friends is fun. But making another kid feel left out is mean.

Bullies want attention. Some believe that bullies use force to get what they want. But what bullies really want is for others to notice them. They get a thrill from attention and power. They want other kids to see that they are confident and in charge.

There are many reasons a kid might be a bully. Sometimes it is to seem tough. Sometimes it is to win friends. Sometimes it is because of jealousy of the kid being bullied. The bully might be being bullied as well.

Getting upset is okay, but taking out your anger on other people is not.

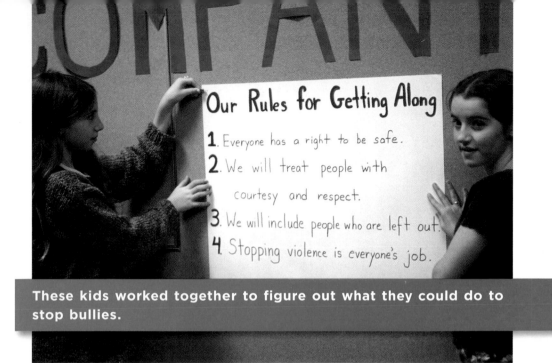

These kids worked together to figure out what they could do to stop bullies.

Change for the Better

Bullying is not a problem that kids can solve alone. Adults must do something about the situation. Here are some suggestions for how to halt bullying.

There are ways to halt bullying. Some schools give kids and parents pamphlets about the problem. They help parents recognize the signs of bullies and bullying. These schools know that all kids are not alike. They encourage kids to celebrate differences, and help kids understand them.

If schools or groups want to stop bullying, they must be relentless. They must encourage peace and discourage bullying every day.

Sometimes a parent can help fix a bullying problem.

Adults do not notice all acts of bullying. Nor will all plans to stop bullying work. Most teachers do stop one kid from hitting another during class. They would also not let kids tease or express unkind thoughts. But adults may not notice bullying in the halls or restrooms.

Scientists say adults only notice four of every one hundred bullying acts. Adults might not always be suspicious of bullies who isolate others. They might not suspect those who act innocently when caught. They might even punish both kids if they just witness a struggle.

People can get together to help stop bullying. Everyone in a school must learn about the problem and be cautious. That means bus drivers, coaches, and lunchroom workers need to be aware. There should be more adults guiding free time to discourage bullying.

Kids who notice bullying can also help to stop it. Most of the time other kids are around when bullying happens. Some kids do not like what they see or hear. Often the whole crowd feels unhappy and afraid. But no one kid wants to stand up to the bully. Kids must work together. Then they might have the courage to stop bullies.

Friends are there for each other – even for the bad times.

Kids cannot learn well if they are being bullied. Stopping bullies can make your school into a better and happier place.

Kids spend a lot of time in school. They are there to learn. Bullies do not belong in the classroom or on the playground.

Teachers, parents, and kids should strive to stop the problem of bullying. Kids need to know that they are safe and secure in school. Those who are bullied should know that it is not their fault. Everyone needs to learn the truth about bullies.

Comprehension Check

Summarize

Read "The Truth About Bullies" again. Then summarize the story.

Think About It

1. Did the author persuade you that bullying is a serious problem? Explain.

Word or Phrase	Technique

2. Why is an injury caused by words as bad as an injury caused by hitting?
3. Do you think having more adults watching kids is a good idea? Why?
4. Reread "The Girl Who Talked to Animals." How is the way Arden was treated similar to how a bully might treat someone? Explain.

Write About It

In many sports, a player who bullies another is taken out of the game. Is this a good way to handle bullying? Why?

Skills and Strategies

Decoding

Decode these words. What do you notice about the spellings?

rope	hugely	untuck	stray
flight	shrink	scratch	flock
replay	smokestack	pressing	airplane

Vocabulary

solo	launch	visible
expedition	tended	permission

Comprehension

MAKE GENERALIZATIONS To make a generalization, use what you know to decide if something is true for a group.

Information from Text	
Prior Knowledge	
Generalization	

A Generalizations Chart helps you make broad statements that describe ideas or events. This will help you organize information and summarize it effectively.

Make a generalization about flying a hot air balloon.

Fly Far, Fly Safely

There is no feeling as grand as flying solo in a hot air balloon. From the moment that the balloon is launched, you feel like you're on top of the world. Huge hills and streams are visible far below. It's incredible!

A hot-air expedition is exciting, but you must still be careful. Balloon pilots need to tend to their equipment. A small rip in their balloon can be dangerous. If the wind changes direction, it can blow a balloon anywhere. There are certain places where balloons are not allowed to fly without permission. When you fly a balloon, be careful and have fun!

Make a **Generalization Chart** for "Fly Far, Fly Safely." Use it to make generalizations about the passage.

Up, Up, and Away!!!

by Rachel Sutton

A Single Clue to Flight

Have you ever watched a campfire burn? Did you see tiny ashes swirl up with the smoke? Years ago, two French brothers watched ashes and smoke rise in their fireplace. The sight of ashes flying up baffled them.

Flight had always interested the men, so they ran a test. First they made little bags using paper. Then the men held the bags upside-down over a fire. Smoke filled the bags and lifted them into the air.

They had to be cautious. If the bags got too close to the fire they burned. The curious brothers tried using larger bags. Smoke lifted the larger bags too!

That summer the brothers made a huge bag, or balloon. They used paper and silk. Their model was forty feet tall. It was as tall as a four-story building!

The men found a place to launch the bag. Then they carefully built a fire under the opening of the bag. Smoke filled the bag up and it rose thousands of feet. The bag cooled quickly. Then an anxious crowd watched it hurtle to the ground.

There was still smoke in the balloon, but it was too cool. To keep the balloon in the air, the smoke had to be hot. The key to balloon flight was heat.

Première ascension d'une montgolfière à Annonay 1783

Townspeople were shocked and excited to see the balloon fly into the sky. They had never seen anything like it before.

Soon the King of France invited the men to the castle. He wanted to see this unique balloon fly. The brothers chose a royal duck, rooster, and sheep as passengers. The men placed the animals in a cage. With a cable, the men attached the cage to the balloon. Helpers lit a fire below the balloon. Smoke filled it up. The balloon lifted the cage and traveled almost two miles. Finally it crashed down.

This expedition gave the men fabulous information. They learned that animals were able to breathe the air up high. They concluded that humans would be able to breathe up high too.

The brothers thought that heavy smoke was the secret to balloon flight. Only later did they find out that the heat was what made the balloon fly.

First in Flight

How long have people been interested in air travel? Look at the year each method of air travel was invented.	
hot air balloon	1783
plane in flight	1903
gasoline powered model plane	1931
jet plane	1939
solar-powered plane in flight	2001
flying car	2002
What's next?	?

For years, people had dreamed of floating away into the sky. This balloon brought that dream to life.

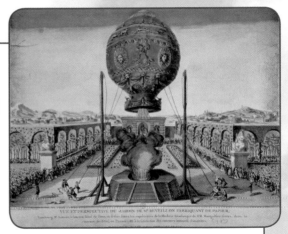

The King gave his permission to try sending people up with the balloon. The brothers made a beautiful blue balloon with a stiff ring around the base. Men would be able to stand in the ring as the balloon rose.

The brothers built a fire low in the neck of the balloon. Smoke filled the balloon. Then two pilots stepped into the balloon's ring. Soon it rose and sailed for miles. The pilots tended the fire. The fabric of the balloon caught on fire, but the men still landed safely.

Balloon pilots have set records since the first balloon journey. The first woman went up in a balloon over two hundred years ago. Soon after, two pilots flew a balloon across the English Channel. That is the large body of water between England and France. Shortly after that, President Washington witnessed the first balloon flight in the United States.

Recently, pilots have set more records. A few years ago, a gas balloon with three pilots crossed the Atlantic Ocean. Then a balloon with four pilots crossed the Pacific Ocean. In 2002 a pilot finally flew solo around the world in a hot air balloon.

Hot air balloon races take place every year, and people come from around the country to join in the fun.

Handling a Hot-Air Balloon

Hot air balloon pilots and passengers often join balloon clubs. Club members plan events like balloon races or trips. Club members often travel to the countryside to find balloon fairs.

A balloon can travel beyond where roads can take us. Passengers enjoy new sights. They might see land or animals that are not visible from the road.

Safety is important. The pilot tells passengers how to handle the balloon. They learn about the parts. Passengers also learn that power lines and trees are unsafe.

The hot air balloon is not a complex machine. Each hot air balloon has an envelope, a propane burner system, and a basket.

The envelope is the cloth balloon. The envelope is often round on top and has an opening at the bottom. It holds in the hot air. The pilot pulls on a cable to open a flap at the top. Then air escapes and the balloon can go down.

The burners sit on a frame below the envelope. Tanks of propane are kept in the basket. The pilot turns on the propane burners to heat air in the balloon.

Passengers ride in the basket. It hangs on the bottom of the frame.

Hot air balloons can go as fast as the wind around them.

Air temperature, wind, and the pilot control the balloon. Warm air always rises above cold air. Warm air in a balloon lifts the balloon above the cooler air outside. When the air in a balloon cools, the balloon sinks.

Wind carries a balloon in flight. A gentle breeze can change a balloon's direction.

A pilot can change a balloon's direction too. Winds at different levels travel in different directions. To go up a level, the pilot turns the gas on. It only takes a few seconds to heat the air. In the stillness, the blast of heat is noisy. To drop to a lower level, the pilot lets the air in the balloon cool.

This pilot carefully changes the amount of hot air that is entering the balloon.

Can you find the basket on *this* hot air balloon?.

Passengers watch other balloons float by in the sky. The designs are different. One balloon might sparkle. Another balloon might be shaped like a pet. Most balloons are round.

The pilot looks for a safe, flat place to land. The balloon seems to dangle before the basket touches the ground. As the basket touches down, the pilot opens the flap to let the hot air out.

Passengers watch the balloon's envelope settle to the ground. The pilot and passengers separate the parts of the balloon. Then they bundle up everything.

The adventure ends. However, someday soon another flight will begin.

Comprehension Check

Summarize

Reread "Up, Up, and Away!!!" Fill in your Generalizations Chart. Then summarize the story.

Information from Text	
Prior Knowledge	
Generalization	

Think About It

1. How are hot-air balloons able to fly?
2. Why is smoke an important detail in the story?
3. Would you like to travel in a balloon? Why or why not?
4. Think about the dangers that faced early hot-air ballooners. Why do you think they chose to try anyway?

Write About It

People have traveled across land, sea, and air to explore the earth. What good things have come from that curiosity? What bad things?

Skills and Strategies

Decoding

Decode these words. What do you notice about the spellings?

robot	peanut	study	mistake
disgusting	reduce	elevator	photograph
shipwreck	triangle	sunlight	passenger

Vocabulary

energy	damage	snatching
chemicals	investigate	request

Comprehension

SEQUENCE The sequence of events is the order in which things happen. Knowing the sequence of events helps you understand the selection.

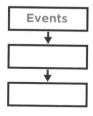

As you read, try to figure out the order of the events in the story. Use a Sequence Chart to show the sequence of events.

Determine the sequence of events.

THE SINKING OF THE TITANIC

The Titanic was said to be a gigantic unsinkable ship. It had a pool, and elevators powered by electric energy. Almost a hundred years ago, it sailed on its first voyage.

Late one night, a block of ice damaged the Titanic. Passengers raced to the lifeboats, snatching children in their arms. The ship sank, and over a thousand passengers drowned.

Today the ship is falling apart because of chemicals and sea animals that eat away at it. Undersea explorers continue to investigate it. They have requested that nothing be taken from the wreck. Who knows what they will discover next?

Make a **Sequence Chart**. Then use it to summarize "The Sinking of the Titanic."

Alvin: Underwater Exploration

by Riley Miller

illustrated by Henry Hull

Beneath the Sea

If you wished to explore a new place, where would you go? Astronauts may fly to the moon to investigate craters and mountains. Adventurers may roam through jungles to find rare plants and animals. Hikers may trek up mountains and explore hot springs or volcanoes.

All of these sights and more are visible on an underwater exploration. Craters and mountains make up the sea floor. Strange plants and interesting animals live there too. Hot springs bubble from the sea floor. Volcanoes gush just like on land.

Alvin is an underwater ship that explores sea floors. Its outer shell looks like a boat. The crew sits in a round cabin in the shell. This cabin is only seven feet wide and completely hidden by the shell. In an emergency, it can separate from the ship. Then it can float like a bubble to the water's surface.

Alvin has two lights attached to it. They are very bright so that the crew can see in the water. Deep underwater, it is very dark because little sunlight reaches that far.

Alvin picks things up with its claws and puts them in baskets. Alvin brings things back to scientists to be studied.

ALVIN

Alvin can only carry three passengers on each trip. There are three small windows in Alvin's walls so that each passenger can see outside. Most passengers are biologists. They study the plants and animals that live deep underwater.

Alvin is launched to sea on the back of a bigger ship. A crane on the ship lowers Alvin into the sea. Alvin falls slowly, like an elevator car. The ship will wait until Alvin is ready to return. Most trips last between six and ten hours.

On the way down, Alvin's passengers can see the water slowly change. It starts off light blue and then slowly dims. As Alvin goes deeper, the water gets darker and darker.

Many fish can't survive or thrive in such dark places. Some fish that live that deep underwater can make their own light. These glowing fish light up just like fireflies. To the passengers on Alvin, the fish look like a light show.

Glowing fish swim deep down, far below the surface. Alvin can go more than twice as deep as those fish. As Alvin gets deeper, the water turns black.

Findings on the Sea Floor

When Alvin reaches the floor, it may find underwater volcanoes called black smokers. Black smokers are made of boiling hot liquid combined with chemicals. The chemical liquid rises from inside the earth. When it hits the icy seawater, it forms a cloud. The chemical in it smells just like rotten eggs. We might find it disgusting, but animals on the sea floor eat it.

These volcanoes look like black smoke coming up from a chimney. That's why scientists call the smoke holes chimneys. Chimneys can be as tall as six-story buildings!

Many animals live near black smokers. They feed on the tiny creatures that eat the chemicals. Those tiny creatures give them energy.

Tube worms are one type of animal that eats these tiny creatures. When tube worms are small, they swallow the creatures. As tube worms grow older, their mouths disappear. The tiny creatures inside of them continue turning chemicals into energy. This makes it so the tube worm can live. Alvin has taken tubeworms back to land by snatching them in its claws. Then scientists can study them.

Alvin can help us find more than just plants and animals. Almost a hundred years ago, a ship named Titanic sank in the sea. People said the ship was unsinkable. On its first trip, it hit a huge chunk of ice and sank. More than one thousand passengers died. Years later, Alvin was sent to find the wreck and photograph it.

The photographs showed the damage after years on the sea floor. The crew placed two metal signs on the wreck during the expedition. One was in memory of those who died. The other was a request that nothing be taken from the wreck.

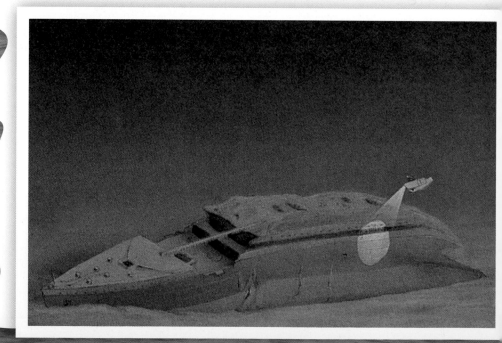

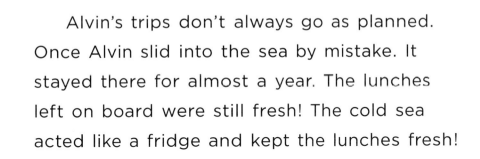

Alvin's trips don't always go as planned. Once Alvin slid into the sea by mistake. It stayed there for almost a year. The lunches left on board were still fresh! The cold sea acted like a fridge and kept the lunches fresh!

On one of Alvin's trips a swordfish attacked the ship! Alvin was on its way to the surface when the fish hit it. Its sharp nose got stuck in Alvin's side. The crew had no way to get rid of the fish. So when Alvin reached the surface, the fish joined them for dinner. It was delicious!

There is much to learn from life underwater. We can learn about the biology of new plants and animals. We can also find out historical information from old shipwrecks. Alvin and its crew can help teach us all these things and more!

Comprehension Check

Summarize

Reread "Alvin: Underwater Exploration." Then summarize the story.

Think About It

1. What can Alvin's passengers see as they go down to the sea floor? How do the sights change with time? Use the Sequence Chart to help you.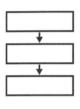

2. Why is it important for the cabin to be able to separate from the rest of the ship? Explain.

3. What would be the most exciting part of a trip in Alvin? What would be the scariest? Why?

4. Reread "Up, Up, and Away!!!" on pages 350-352. How is a balloon flight like an underwater expedition? How is it different?

✏ Write About It

Do you think the underwater explorations in Alvin are important? Why or why not?

Skills and Strategies

TITLE	DECODING	VOCABULARY	COMPREHENSION
Unit 1 pages 6-65			
6 Dan Can Rap	/a/a p<u>a</u>ck, /e/e s<u>e</u>t, /i/i sp<u>i</u>ll, /o/o st<u>o</u>p, /u/u m<u>u</u>d	hand, nervous, slips, worried, gasps, on edge	Analyze Story Structure: Character, Plot
18 Jane Wins a Job	/ā/a_e s<u>ame</u>, /ē/e_e th<u>ese</u>, /ī/i_e l<u>ike</u>, /ō/o_e st<u>ove</u> /ū/u_e t<u>une</u>	create, logging, awoke, enormous, smokestack	Analyze Story Structure: Setting, Plot
30 Do They Make You Shudder and Shake?	/f/ph <u>ph</u>one; /sh/sh bru<u>sh</u>; /th/th wi<u>th</u>; /hw/ wh <u>wh</u>en	stun, prey, venom, reptile, victim	Analyze Text Structure: Compare and Contrast
42 Seeing Mars	/ē/e sh<u>e</u>, ee s<u>ee</u>m, ea dr<u>ea</u>m, y happ<u>y</u>	orbits, object, volcano, gravity	Generate Questions: Summarize
54 Ray and Blaine Save the Day	/ā/ay st<u>ay</u>, ai m<u>ai</u>n, a b<u>a</u>by	plea, supplies, dismay, beam recover, cure	Generate Questions: Cause and Effect
Unit 2 pages 66-125			
66 The Problem with Sy	/ī/i qu<u>i</u>et, y tr<u>y</u>, igh s<u>igh</u>t	fierce, fright, trembling, perch, escapes	Monitor Comprehension: Make Inferences
78 Large Trees with Large Jobs	/s/c spa<u>c</u>e, /j/g pa<u>g</u>e	gems, ripen, protect, disputes, concerned	Summarize: Main Idea and Details
90 Which Way to Freedom?	/ch/ch whi<u>ch</u>, tch pa<u>tch</u>	citizens, succeeded, dedicated, relief, advised	Summarize: Main Idea and Details
102 Joan's First Parade	/ō/o f<u>o</u>cus, oa b<u>oa</u>t	excitement, costumes, refused, fabric, shrieked boasted	Summarize: Problem and Solution
114 A Cowboy's Life	/ou/ow br<u>ow</u>n, ou r<u>ou</u>nd	prowling, daring, swiftly, roaming, well-rounded	Monitor Comprehension: Make Inferences
Unit 3 pages 126-185			
126 A Ride in the Moonlight	/ü/oo b<u>oo</u>t	country, sign, idea, swooped, patriots	Make Inferences and Analyze: Draw Conclusions
138 Susan B. Anthony: Making Her Mark on the Women's Rights Movement	/är/ar st<u>ar</u>t	delay, basis, committee, grant, offended, regarding	Evaluate: Fact and Opinion
150 A Place for Us to Breathe	/ôr/or f<u>or</u>, ore st<u>ore</u>	lantern, fortunately, declared, exposed, fragile	Evaluate: Fact and Opinion
162 A Desert Vacation	/ûr/er h<u>er</u>, ir f<u>ir</u>st, ur s<u>ur</u>f	fret, remarkable, unique images, echoes	Make Inferences and Analyze: Compare and Contrast
174 Hope's Trip to Planet Wren	/n/kn <u>kn</u>ow, /r/wr <u>wr</u>ite, /mb/b lam<u>b</u>	wreck, combing, variety, knoll, seized, grave	Make Inferences and Analyze: Draw Conclusions

TITLE	DECODING	VOCABULARY	COMPREHENSION
Unit 4 pages 186-245			
186 Grandpop's Brave Choice	/oi/oi s<u>oi</u>l, oy b<u>oy</u>	confidence, assured, offices, confused, accept	Analyze Story Structure: Character, Setting
198 Big Ideas for Little Animals	/əl/el ang<u>el</u>, le bubb<u>le</u>	survive, injure, attempts odor, ordinarily,	Evaluate: Author's Purpose
210 A New Government	/ô/au p<u>au</u>se, aw cl<u>aw</u>, /ôl/al salt	developed, structure, foolishly, authored, absolute	Evaluate: Make Generalizations
222 Follow the Weather	/ō/o t<u>o</u>ld, ow <u>ow</u>n, oa b<u>oa</u>t	shelter, destroyed, dense, quarrel, treacherous	Analyze Text Structure: Description
234 Brook's Vase of Good Thoughts	/ủ/oo b<u>oo</u>k	revolves, filthy, common, product, introduction	Evaluate: Author's Purpose
Unit 5 pages 246-305			
246 The Loneliest Place on Earth	Review: /ā/ and /a/	extreme, frequently, harsh, inhabited, contacting, enables	Generate Questions: Problem and Solution
258 The Perfect Ingredient	Review: /ī/ and /i/	miserable, eager, grumbled, suggested, compressed	Make Inferences and Analyze: Theme
270 Plants That Can Heal	Review: /ē/ and /e/	preparation, reduce, available, scents, precise	Make Inferences and Analyze: Cause and Effect
282 Joe and Nicole Crack the Code	Review: /ō/ and /o/	inappropriate, treasure, situations, irregular, impatiently	Generate Questions: Evaluate Author's Perspective
294 Proof of Goodness	Review: /ü/ and /ủ/	vanished, reflection, majesty, depend, delicious	Generate Questions: Summarize
Unit 6 pages 306-365			
306 The Girl Who Talked to Animals	ər/er ev<u>er</u> , əl/el/ tunn<u>el</u>, ən/en/ wood<u>en</u>	peculiar, innocent, communicate, bustling, deserve	Summarize: Identify Sequence of Events
318 An Outdoor Adventure	Review: /ou/ou r<u>ou</u>nd, ow br<u>ow</u>n and /ō/	surrounded, secure, concluded, scuttle, eerie	Monitor Comprehension: Make Judgments
330 The Truth About Bullies	Review: /th/th wi<u>th</u>, /sh/ sh <u>sh</u>ip, /hw/wh <u>wh</u>en, /f/ph gra<u>ph</u>	anxious, gestures, thrive, halt, witness	Monitor Comprehension: Identify Techniques of Persuasion
342 Up, Up, and Away!!!	Review: long vowels and short vowels	tended, launch, expedition, solo, permission, visible	Monitor Comprehension: Make Generalizations
354 Alvin: Underwater Exploration	Review: long vowels and short vowels	investigate, energy, chemicals, damage, snatching, request	Summarize: Identify Sequence of Events

ACKNOWLEDGMENTS

ILLUSTRATIONS

7-16: Tomoko Watanabe.19-28: Dana Trattner. 55-64: Maureen Zimdars. 67-76: Shelly Shinjo. 91-100: James E. Seward. 103-112: Tyrone Geter. 127-136: Rick Powell. 139-148: Chris Peterson. 151-160: David Rankin. 163-172: Shelly Hehenberger. 175-184: Karel Hayes. 189-196: Michael Hobbs. 235-244: Catherine Huerta. 259-268: Christy Hale. 283-292: Cathy Morrison. 295-304: Dennis Albetski. 307-316: John Hovell. 319-328: Nancy J. Staroski. 355-364: Henry Hill.

PHOTOGRAPHY

All photographs are by Macmillan/McGraw Hill (MMH) except as noted below:

3: (tr) Peter Arnold, Inc./Alamy; (cr) Claus Meyer/Getty Images; (br) Stuart Dee/Getty Images; 4: (bl) Brand X Pictures/Punchstock; 5: (tr) david tipling/Alamy; (br) Ethel Davies/imagestate/PictureQuest; 31: Santiago Fdez Fuentes/AGEfotostock; 32: Claus Meyer/Getty Images; 33: (t) Douglas Peebles Photography/Alamy; (b) Morales/AGEfotostock; 34: Niall Benvie/CORBIS; 35: Jack Milchanowski/AGEfotostock; 36: Sylvain Cordier/Peter Arnold, Inc.; 37: Santiago Fdez Fuentes/AGEfotostock; 38: David A. Northcott/CORBIS; 39: Steve Hamblin/Alamy; 40: Sylvain Cordier/Peter Arnold, Inc.; 43: Peter Arnold, Inc./Alamy; 44: Peter Arnold, Inc./Alamy; 45: Getty Images; 46: (inset) David A. Hardy/Photo Researchers, Inc.; 46-47: NASA/JPL/CORBIS; 48: (bkgd) Brand X Pictures/Punch Stock; (inset) NASA/JPL/CORBIS; 49: John R. Foster/Photo Researchers, Inc.; 50: SuperStock/AGEfotostock; 51: © 1989 Roger Ressmeyer/NASA/CORBIS; 52: Richard T. Nowitz/CORBIS; 79: Edward Parker/Alamy; 80: Stuart Dee/Getty Images; 81: Danita Delimont/Alamy; 82: Digital Vision/Punchstock; 83: Edward Parker/Alamy; 84: Edward Parker/Alamy; 85: Comstock Images/Alamy; 86: Image Source/Alamy; 87: Westend61/Alamy; 88: Raymond Gehman/CORBIS; 91: © Royalty-Free/CORBIS; 93: Bettmann/CORBIS; 94: SuperStock, Inc./SuperStock; 96: The Granger Collection, New York; 98: Louie Psihoyos/CORBIS; 100: Bettmann/CORBIS; 115: Bettmann/CORBIS; 116: Nebraska State Historical Society Photograph Collections; 117: The Art Archive/Bill Manns; 118: The Art Archive/Bill Manns; 119: Bettmann/CORBIS; 120: The Art Archive/Bill Manns; 121: Bettmann/CORBIS; 122: CORBIS; 123: CORBIS; 124: The Granger Collection, New York; 151: © Comstock/PunchStock; 156: Medioimages/Alamy; 162: S Wanke/Photolink; 166: Creatas/Punchstock; 167: John A Rizzo/Getty Images; 199: Comstock/PunchStock; 200: James Warwick/Getty Images; 201: J Sneesby/B Wilkins/Getty Images; 202: Index Stock Imagery/PictureQuest; 203: Comstock/PunchStock; 204: Neal and Molly Jansen/Alamy; 205: Frans Lanting/Minden Pictures; 206: Reinhard Dirscherl/Alamy; 207: Anthony Banister/Gallo Images/CORBIS; 208: StockTrek/Getty Images; 211: © Joseph Sohm/Visions of America/CORBIS; 212: The Granger Collection, New York; 213: SuperStock, Inc./SuperStock; 214: SuperStock, Inc./SuperStock; 215: © Joseph Sohm/Visions of America/CORBIS; 216: Wally McNamee/CORBIS; 217: Ron Sachs/CORBIS; 218: Brooks Kraft/CORBIS; 219: Bettmann/CORBIS; 220: Jeff Greenberg/Alamy; 224: Dennis MacDonald/Alamy; 225: Brand X Pictures/Punchstock; 226: G. Rossenbach/zefa/Corbis; 227: Jason Hosking/zefa/Corbis; 228: Jeff Smith/Alamy; 229: Eric Nguyen/Jim Reed Photography/CORBIS; 230: © Royalty-Free/Corbis; 231: Alaska Stock LLC/Alamy; 232: RICK WILKING/Reuters/Corbis; 247: Daryl Benson/Masterfile; 248: Geosphere/Planetary Visions/Photo Researchers, Inc.; (bkgd) © Creatas/PunchStock; 249: Royal Geographical Society/Alamy; (bkgd) © Creatas/PunchStock; 250: Daryl Benson/Masterfile; (bkgd) © Creatas/PunchStock; 251: Galen Rowell/CORBIS; 252: david tipling/Alamy; (bkgd) © Creatas/PunchStock; 253: Bill Bachmann/Photo Researchers, Inc.; (bkgd) © Creatas/PunchStock; 254: Maria Stenzel/National Geographic/Getty Images; (bkgd) © Creatas/PunchStock; 255: Bob Krist/CORBIS; (bkgd) © Creatas/PunchStock; 256: Ben Osborne/Getty Images; 272-273: John E Marriott/Alamy; 273: Peter Arnold, Inc./Alamy; 274: Chuck Brown/Photo Researchers, Inc.; 274-275: Chris Cheadle/Getty Images; 276: R.O. - Photosure.com/AGEfotostock; 277: Ed Reschke/Peter Arnold, Inc.; 278: Michael Gadomski/Photo Researchers, Inc.; 279: Peter M. Wilson/CORBIS; 280: Edward Parker/Alamy; 332: Will & Deni McIntyre/CORBIS; 333: Michelle D. Bridwell/Photo Edit; 334: Lawrence Migdale/Photo Researchers, Inc.; 335: Ray Pietro/Photonica/Getty Images; 336: Amy Etra/Photo Edit; 337: David Young-Wolff/Photo Edit; 338: Gideon Mendel/CORBIS; 339: David Young-Wolff/Photo Edit; 340: PHOTOTAKE Inc./Alamy; 343: Ethel Davies/imagestate/PictureQuest; 344: © Ken Chernus/Getty Images; 344-345: (bkgd) PhotoLink/Getty Images; 345: (br) Science Museum Pictorial/Science & Society Picture Library; 346: (br) Sheila Terry/Photo Researchers, Inc.; 346-347: (bkgd) PhotoLink/Getty Images; 347: (cr) AKG/Photo Researchers, Inc.; 348: (tl) TONY ASHBY/AFP/Getty Images; (r) Trevor Collens-Pool/Getty Images; 348-349: (bkgd) PhotoLink/Getty Images; 349: (t) Jay S Simon/Getty Images; 350: (tr) PhotoLink/Getty Images; (br) Ethel Davies/imagestate/PictureQuest; 350-351: (bkgd) PhotoLink/Getty Images; 351: (br) Travel Ink/Alamy; 352: (t) Tony Cunningham/Alamy; (bkgd) PhotoLink/Getty Images.